THE GREAT BIG BOOK OF MATHS

ON OUR WAY

QED Publishing

First published in the UK in 2008 by
QED Publishing
A Quarto Group company
226 City Road
London EC1V 2TT

www.qed-publishing.co.uk

A Catalogue record for this book is available from the British Library.

ISBN 978 1 84835 097 7

Written by Ann Montague-Smith
Illustrated by Peter Lawson
Photography by Steve Lumb

Publisher: Steve Evans
Creative Director: Zeta Davies

Printed and bound in China

Contents

ADDING AND SUBTRACTING

Using Numbers

Counting to 20

Match the numbers to the bugs.

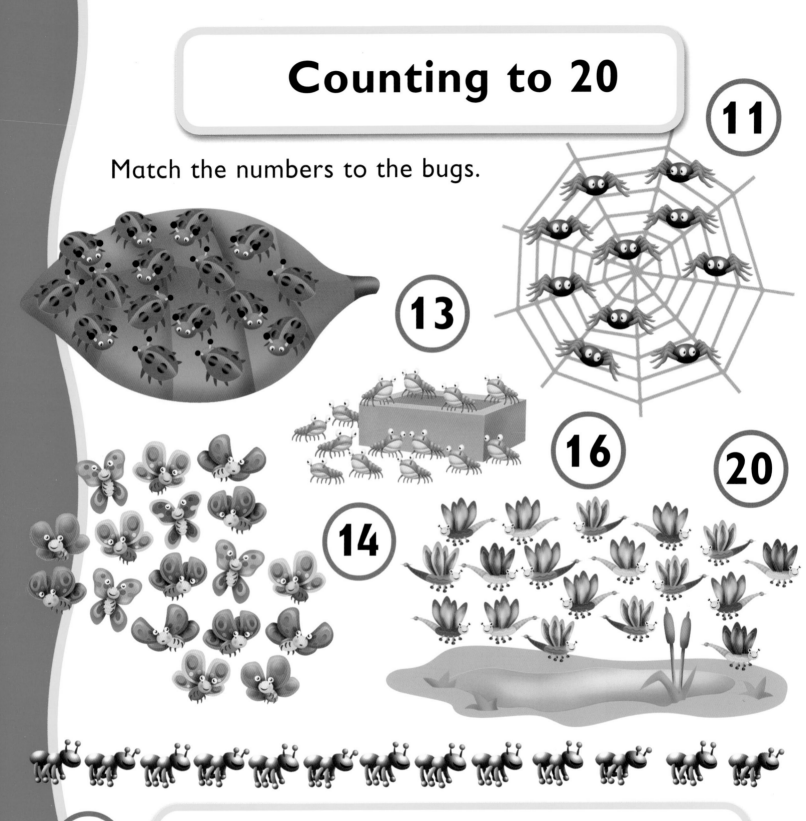

11

13

16

20

14

19

What if there were 1 more in each set. How many would there be then? How many would there be if there were 1 fewer in each set?

18

15

Try this

Take turns with a friend to get an armful of toys. Ask your friend to count the toys. Now you count them. Do you agree? Make piles of toys for 10, 13, 15... up to 20.

10

12

17

Estimating

You will need a pile of 30 counters. Take a big handful of counters from the pile and put them onto the carpet below. Guess how many there are. Now count them to check.

Do this 5 more times.

Now try this

Use handfuls of straws instead of counters. Estimate and count to check. Do this five more times.

Numbers to 30

Play this game with a friend. You will need a 1–6 dice and a counter each. Take turns to roll the dice. Move your counter that number of spaces. Say the number where your counter lands. The winner is the first one to reach the finish.

Start

1 2 3 4 5 6 7 8 9 10 11 12 13 14 15

Play the game again. This time, start at the end and work backwards along the track.

Try this

Choose a book and look at the page numbers. Copy the numbers onto some paper. Can you read and write all the numbers up to 40?

16 17 18 19 20 21 22 23 24 25 26 27 28 29 30

Finish

Place value

Throw a coin onto the spinner. Take that number of counters and put them on the Ones planet. When you have 10 counters on the Ones planet, take these away and put one counter on the Tens planet. Say each time how many tens and how many ones you have, then say the whole number. Keep going until you have two counters on the Tens planet.

Tens

Do this again. This time go to 3 Tens.

spinner

1	2
4	3

Challenge

You will need some playing cards. Take out all the picture cards. Shuffle the rest of the cards. Say any number between 10 and 40. Now use the cards to make the number.

36

Ones

15

Counting patterns

Start at 0. Count along the track in 2s.
Which numbers do you say?

4 5 6 7 8

3

2

1

0

Start

What if you counted in 5s? And 10s? And 3s?
Write a list of the numbers that you say.

Find out

What if you counted in 2s starting on 14 and ending on 26? What numbers would you say? Now count back in 2s from 28 to 18. What numbers would you say? Now try counting on in 5s from 10. How far can you count?

14, 16, 18, 20...

9 10 11 12 13 14 15 16 17 18 19 20 Finish

17

Odds and evens

The gardener planted some flower bulbs in even numbers. The rabbits ate some of the bulbs. Which rows have even numbers of flowers?

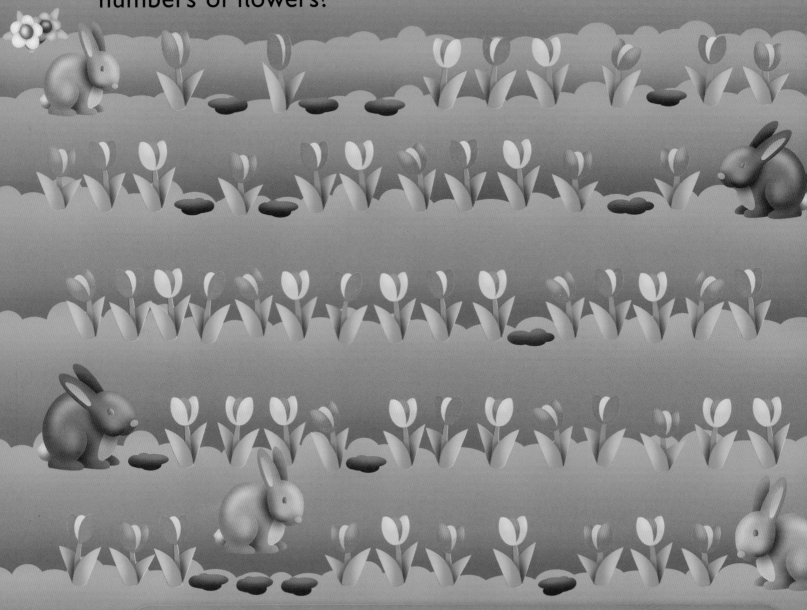

Add 1 to the number of flowers in each row. Now which rows have even numbers of flowers?

18

What if you add two flowers to each row? Which would be even now? Which would be odd? What if you added three flowers?

Making comparisons

Decide which home has more in each pair of sets below.
Say how many more there are.

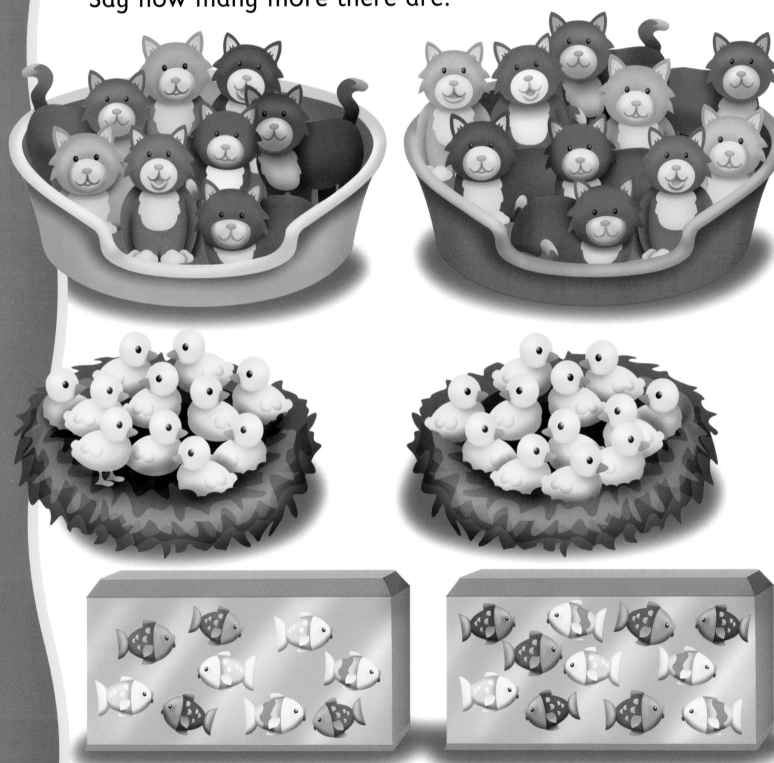

Count each set of animals below:
Say the number that is 1 more.
Say the number that is 1 less.
Say the number that is 10 more.
Say the number that is 10 less.

Now try this

Choose a page in this book between
11 and 24. Say its page number.
Now say these numbers: 1 more,
1 less, 10 more and 10 less.
Try this again for another page.
You could write your numbers down.

15
16, 14
25, 5

Ordering numbers to 20

Look at the lines of numbers. The numbers are in order, but the bears have dropped paint onto some of the numbers. Which numbers have paint on them?

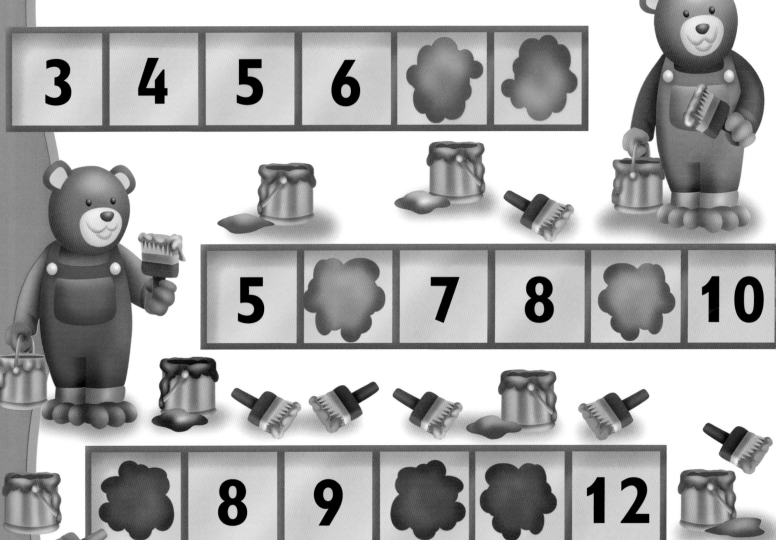

| 3 | 4 | 5 | 6 | | |

| 5 | | 7 | 8 | | 10 |

| | 8 | 9 | | | 12 |

Two of the number grids on these pages could be placed together to make a longer line of numbers in order. Which grids are those? Write the numbers down in order.

Challenge

You will need some playing cards. Take out all the face cards. Choose two cards. Put them in number order. Now say a number which would fit between your numbers.

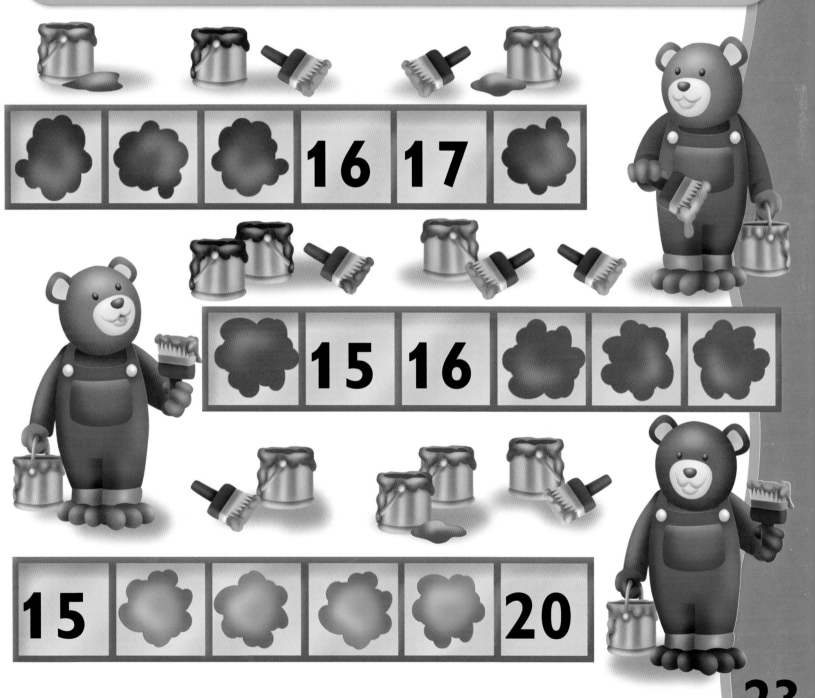

| | | | **16** | **17** | |

| | **15** | **16** | | | |

| **15** | | | | | **20** |

Number problems

You will need some counters in two different colours. Jump your finger along the track in 2s. Put a counter on each number that you touch. Do this again for jumps of 3s. Write a list of the numbers that have 2 counters on them. What is special about these numbers?

Now try this

Jump along the track in 5s. Put a counter on each number that you touch. Now think about jumping along the track in 2s. Can you guess which numbers would be touched by jumps of both 2 and 5?

5, 10, 15...

2, 4, 6, 8, 10...

16 17 18 15 19 14 20 21 22 23 24 25 26 27 28 29 30

Finish

Numbers to 100

Play this game with a friend. Take turns to throw a small coin onto the spinner. Move your counter that number, on the windows of the buildings. Say the number you land on out loud.

Start

1	2	3	4
5	6	7	8
9	10	11	12
13	14	15	16
17	18	19	20
21	22		

23	24	25
26	27	28
29	30	31
32	33	34
35	36	37

38	39	40	41
42	43	44	45
46	47	48	49
50	51	52	53
54	55	56	57
		58	59
		60	61

Take turns to point to any number.
Ask your friend to say it.

spinner

1 2
3 4

Try this

With a friend, take turns to say a number between 1 and 99. Now decide whether to count up to 100 from that number, or down to 0. Now write that number, and the next nine numbers, in order.

Start at 45 and count back.

62	63	64	65
66	67	68	69
70	71	72	73
74	75	76	77
78	79	80	81

82	83	84	85
86	87	88	89
90	91	92	93
94	95	96	97
98	99		100

Finish

Counting to 100

The dogs have spilt paint on the number strips.
Can you work out which numbers are missing?

0 1 2 3 ▓ ▓ 6

7 8 ▓ ▓ 11 12 13

▓ ▓ ▓ ▓ 18 19 20

28 29 30 ▓ ▓ ▓ 34

Say the numbers for each number strip in reverse order.

Now try this

Say all the numbers from 0 to 100. Now count backwards, starting with 100, 99, 98...

100, 99, 98, 97, 96, 95, 94...

50

62 63 64 ❀ ❀ 67 ❀

79 ❀ ❀ ❀ ❀ 84

❀ 90 ❀ ❀ 93 ❀

95 ❀ ❀ 98 ❀ 100

Tens and units

Match the tens and units balloons to the items of food.

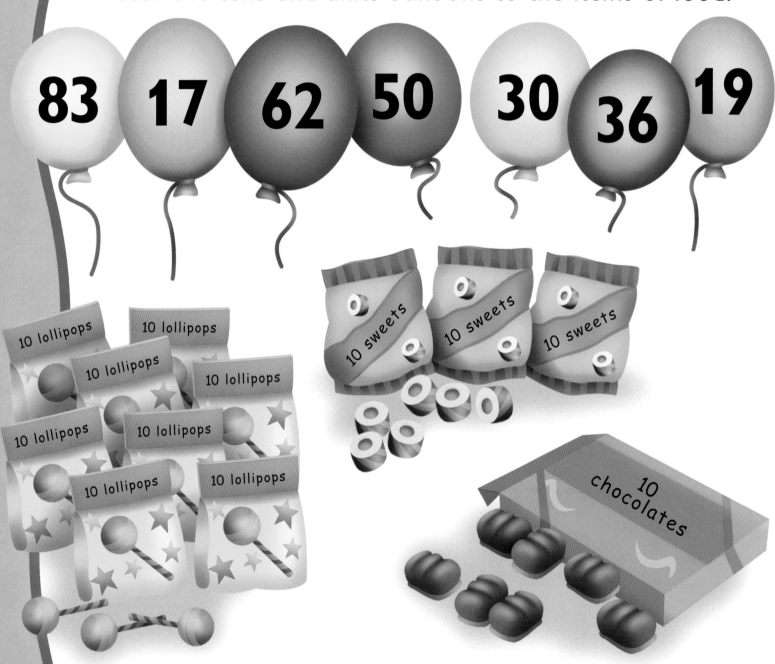

83 17 62 50 30 36 19

10 lollipops

10 sweets

10 chocolates

Which is the largest tens and units number?
Which is the smallest?

10 biscuits

10 biscuits

10 bisuits

10 biscuits

10 biscuits

10 biscuits

Tens and Units (TU) numbers can be written like this: 34=30+4. Think of five more TU numbers. Write them like this.

34=30+4

10 lemons

10 lemons

10 lemons

10 lemons

10 lemons

10 cupcakes

10 cupcakes

10 cupcakes

10 apples

Counting on or back

Choose a number from the carpet below. Count on from that number to 100, then back again.

1	2	3	4	5
11	12	13	14	15
21	22	23	24	25
31	32	33	34	35
41	42	43	44	45
51	52	53	54	55
61	62	63	64	65
71	72	73	74	75
81	82	83	84	85
91	92	93	94	95

Choose some more numbers and do it again.

Challenge

Count on from 100.
How far can you count?
Can you count back to 100?

100, 101, 102, 103, 104, 105, 106...

6	7	8	9	10
16	17	18	19	20
26	27	28	29	30
36	37	38	39	40
46	47	48	49	50
56	57	58	59	60
66	67	68	69	70
76	77	78	79	80
86	87	88	89	90
96	97	98	99	100

Ordering numbers to 100

Some of the t-shirts have lost their numbers.
Look at the numbers on the ground.
Which numbers will fit in the spaces on the t-shirts?

Which number will not fit? Can you explain why?

Try this

You will need some playing cards. Take out the face cards. Take two cards. Make a TU number with them. Now make another TU number with your cards. Write as many numbers as you can that will fit between your two numbers.

29

37

41

84

22

60

5

73

49

18

50

More or less

Read the numbers on the labels. Say the number that is **1** more than each number. Now say the number that is **1** less than each number.

Do this again. This time say the 10 more and 10 less numbers.

51

36

Challenge

Write down any number between 30 and 80. Now write down the number that is 20 more. Write down the number that is 20 less. Now write all your numbers in order, starting with the smallest number.

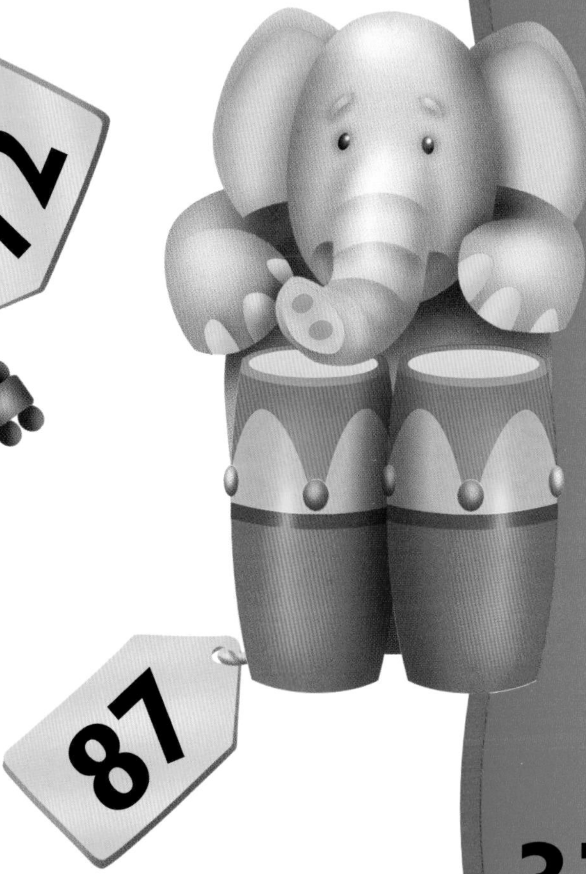

18 38 58

72

48

87

37

Missing numbers

Some of the numbers have fallen off this piece of a hundred square that Gerry Giraffe is holding. Which ones?

	2	3	4
11	12	13	14
21	22	23	24
	32	33	

5	6	7	8
15	16	17	18
	26	27	
	36	37	
		47	

31			
41	42	43	44
51		53	
61	62	63	

		83			
	92	93	94	95	96	97

Now look at the pieces of the hundred square the other animals are holding. Work out which numbers are missing.

Now try this

Mark with a pencil a 10 by 10 grid on some squared paper. Write 1 in the top left-hand corner square, and 100 in the bottom right-hand corner square. Take turns to write in any number on the grid until all the numbers from 1 to 100 are there in order.

The elephant's grid:

				64	65
	72	73		74	75
81	82				
				84	85

The main 100-grid:

1	2	3	4	5	6	7	8	9	10
11	12	13	14	15	16	17	18	19	20
21	22	23	24	25	26	27	28	29	30
31	32	33	34	35	36	37	38	39	40
41	42	43	44	45	46	47	48	49	50
51	52	53	54	55	56	57	58	59	60
61	62	63	64	65	66	67	68	69	70
71	72	73	74	75	76	77	78	79	80
81	82	83	84	85	86	87	88	89	90
91	92	93	94	95	96	97	98	99	100

The tiger's grid:

45	46		
55	56	57	58
	66	67	68
		77	78
		87	88

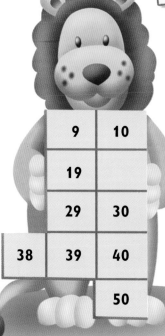

The lion's grid:

9	10
19	
29	30
38	39	40
	50

The second tiger's grid:

48	49	
	59	
	69	70
		80
	89	90
98	99	100

39

Rounding

Numbers with units from 1 to 4 round down to the nearest 10. Numbers with units from 5 to 9 round up to the nearest 10. Round the numbers on the apples.

Write all the numbers on the apples in order. Write underneath the number that each apple number will round to.

Now try this

This girl wants to buy 35 sweets to share with the children in her class. The sweets come in packs of 10. How many packs of sweets must she buy? Suppose there were 32 children in her class. How many packs of sweets would she need now? Explain your answer to a friend.

82

57

14

65

78

43

19

24

92

84

Path problem

The numbers on the path must be painted on. The first slab reads '1'. The last slab will read '99', so this will need two 9s to be painted. How many number 1s need to be painted? How many number 2s, 3s, 4s, 5s, 6s, 7s, 8s and 9s?

Can you find a quick way to work this out?

10
9
8
7

90
91
92
93
94
95
96
97
98
99

Challenge

What if the numbers went from 51 to 150? How many of each digit would be needed?

Supporting notes for adults

Counting to 20 – pages 8–9

Count with real objects at first, then move to counting pictures.
Extend this to counting sets to 30, then beyond. Try to use lots of different contexts.

Estimating – pages 10–11

Use different objects for estimating and counting, e.g. coins, cubes, counters, etc,
so that the children experience estimating items of various sizes.
Try putting small things, such as marbles and buttons, into a transparent container,
and ask the children to estimate these. Use pictures in books.
Give the children a few seconds to look, then close the book and ask,
'How many… do you think there were?'

Numbers to 30 – pages 12–13

Provide opportunities for reading and writing numbers up to at least 30, such as finding page
numbers in books; reading numbers on packaging; prices, etc. Encourage the children to write the
numbers in the air with their arms, so that they 'feel' the shape that the numbers make.

Place value – pages 14–15

Exchange games can be played with coins, e.g. 1s and 10s coins. Ask the child to take a
handful of 1 coins and to count these out. Then exchange 10 one coins for a 10 coin.
Then ask, 'How much money do you have?' Children can use playing cards to make TU
(tens and units) numbers. They read the number and say how many tens and how many units.

Counting patterns – pages 16–17

Practise saying the patterns for counting in 2s from 0 to 20 and back again.
Do this for 5s, 10s and 3s up to about 30. When children are confident with this,
they can say the patterns backward, starting with 20, then 30.
Children may like to sing the counting patterns to music.

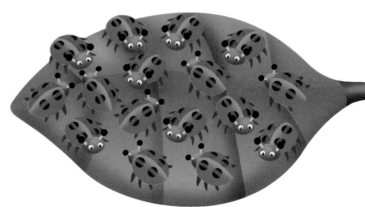

Odds and evens – pages 18–19

Where children are counting objects, they can pair these to see if they are even
(pairs with no odd ones) or odd (always 1 left over).
Encourage children to recognize that even numbers always have 0, 2, 4, 6, or 8
in their unit number, and that odd numbers always have 1, 3, 5, 7, or 9.

Making comparisons – pages 20–21

Children can compare numbers that they find around them, such as numbers in books,
on toys, etc. They can say, of two numbers, which is more/less, and what number(s)
could fit between them. Encourage them to say numbers that are 1 more/less than
any number up to 30, and for numbers between 10 and 20, numbers that are 10 more/less.

Ordering numbers to 20 – pages 22–23

Ask questions about number order such as, 'Which numbers could fit between… and…?'
If children are unsure, use some number cards so that they can find the numbers
they need and place these in order.

Number problems – 24–25

This number investigation encourages children to think about how
some numbers come in both the counts of 2 and of 3. This is the basis of the 6 times table,
of course. If children find the jumping along the track difficult,
suggest that they use their fingers to keep track of each jump of 2 or 3.

Numbers to 100 – pages 26–27

Encourage children to read the numbers and to write them. Point to any number and check
that the children can read it. If they are unsure, discuss the tens number, then the units number,
then the whole number, so that the child begins to understand how the number is made up.

Counting to 100 – pages 28–29

If children are unsure about numbers larger than about 30, count together
from 0 to 100 and back again, several times. Now point to the numbers on the page
and read these together, so that children become more confident
with the numbers before tackling the task.

Tens and units – pages 30–31

As well as being able to read and write tens and units numbers, children need to understand what each of the digits stand for. If children are unsure about this, read the tens and units numbers in two ways. For example, take 25: 2 tens and 5 units is the same as twenty-five.

Counting on or back – pages 32–33

If children are unsure about counting to 100, then they can make mistakes such as twenty-nine, twenty-ten, twenty-eleven. Check that the children understand what to say at the decade change: 29, 30… 39, 40… and so forth.

Ordering numbers to 100 – pages 34–35

If children are unsure about which numbers could fit in the spaces, count on from the smaller number to the larger number. This will help children to realize which numbers could fit.

More or less – pages 36–37

If children find this activity difficult, ask them to write out the numbers from 1 to 100, or do this for them, in a grid with 1–10 along the first line, 11–20 along the next and so forth, lining up the numbers. Use this to find the 1 more and 1 less numbers, then the 10 more and 10 less numbers. Ask 'What do you notice about 10 more? And 10 less? Where do these come on the grid?'

Missing numbers – pages 38–39

Children may find it easier to tackle this activity with a full hundred square grid, with 1 in the top left-hand corner, and 100 in the bottom right-hand corner. When they are confident with using this, ask them to try the activity again, this time without the hundred square grid.

Rounding – pages 40–41

As long as children understand the convention that units of 5–9 round up, and 1–4 round down, rounding is easy. If children do find it difficult, suggest that they write the numbers 1 to 9 in order, and draw a line between 4 and 5. They can use their line to help them remember which numbers round up, and which down.

Path problem – pages 42–43

Nineteen of each of 1, 2, 3,… 9 will be needed. Discourage children from just counting each digit. Instead, suggest that they look at the numbers 1–9, then 11–20, then 21–30, to see how many of each digit is used. Encourage them to predict from what they notice about the overall total for each digit.

Adding and Subtracting

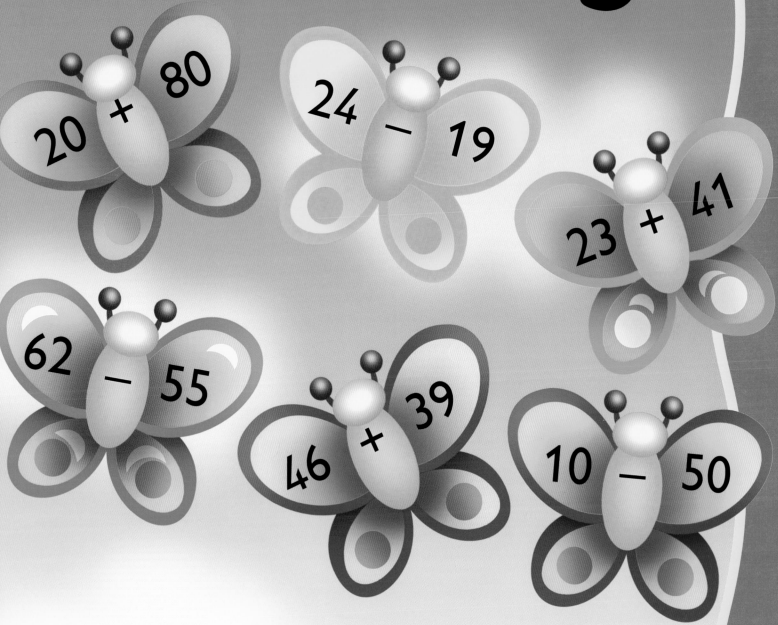

$20 + 80$

$24 - 19$

$23 + 41$

$62 - 55$

$46 + 39$

$10 - 50$

Counting on

Look at each of the two sets of cats. Find the larger set and count how many. Keep that number in your head and count on for the smaller set. What number do you get to?

set 1

set 2

set 1

set 2

Which sets total 9?

set 1

set 2

Challenge

You will need 9 counters. How many different ways can you find to make two sets which total 9? Write some addition sentences using + and = to show what you have found.

1+8=9

set 1

set 2

set 1

set 2

49

Adding small numbers

Which two sets add up to 8? Find out by counting on in ones from the larger number. How many different ways can you find to do this?

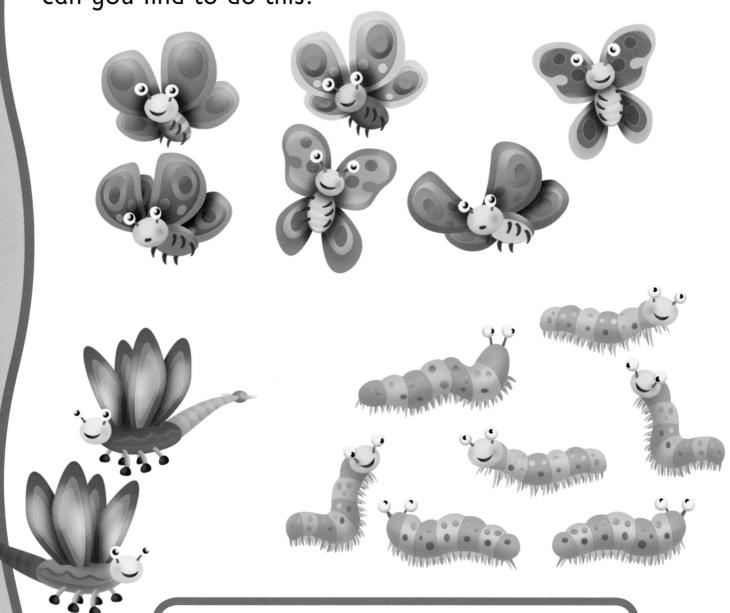

Which 3 sets add up to 12?
Find 3 different ways to do this.

Now try this

Add four sets together. What different totals can you make? Write them as addition sentences. Use + and = like this.

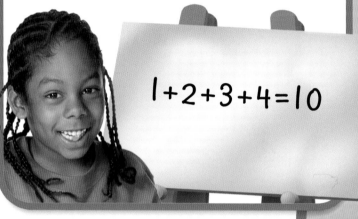

$1+2+3+4=10$

51

Totals of 10

Find two sets which total 10.

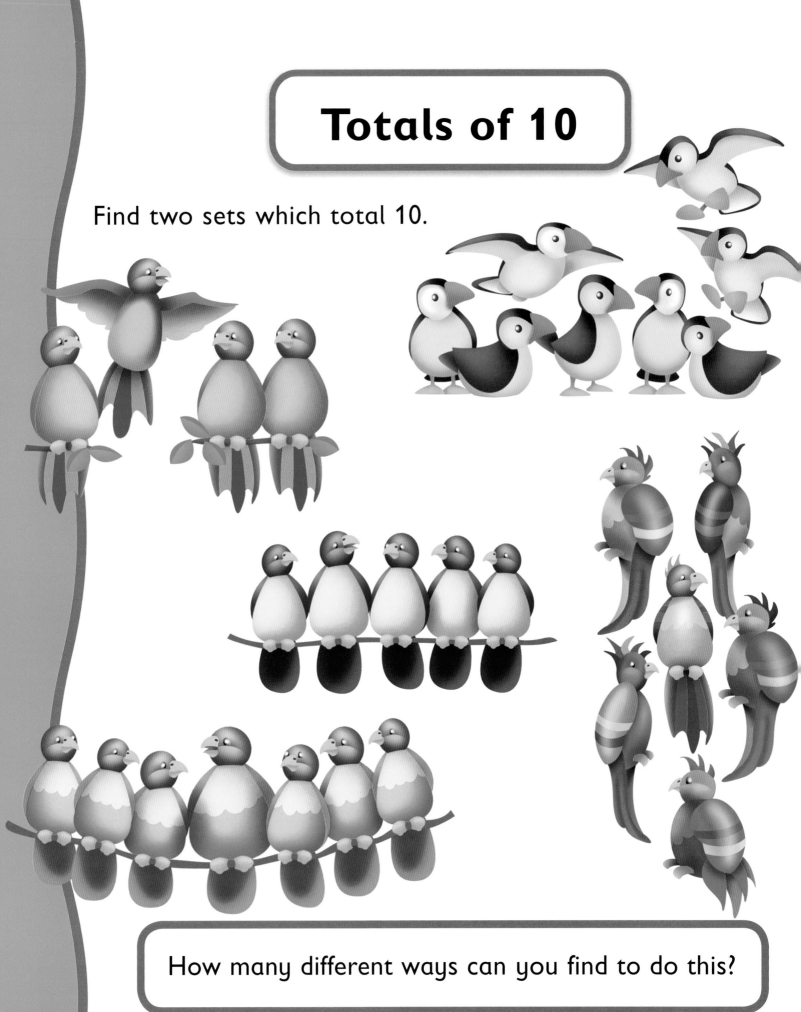

How many different ways can you find to do this?

52

Now try this

You will need 10 counters and a friend.
Take some of the counters.
Don't tell your friend how many you have.
Now ask your friend to look at what is
left. Can he/she say how many you took?
Now swap over.

Adding to 10

Play this game with a friend. You will need some counters in two colours. Take turns to choose a number from both circle 1 and circle 2. Add the numbers together. Cover your answer on the bears' picnic blanket with a counter. The winner is the one with the most counters on the blanket.

Play again, but this time choose two numbers each time from the picnic blanket which you think total 10. Cover both numbers with counters if you are correct.

Use a 1-6 dice.
Throw the dice twice.
Write an addition sentence with the two numbers using + and =. Do this 4 times.

6+3=9

6

5

8

7

5

7

8

3

9

4

9

4

Doubles and near doubles

Play this game with a friend. You will need a 1–6 dice and two counters. Take turns to throw the dice. Move that number on the track. Work out the answer to the addition sentence. If you get it wrong, move your counter back to where you were. The winner is the first one to the finish.

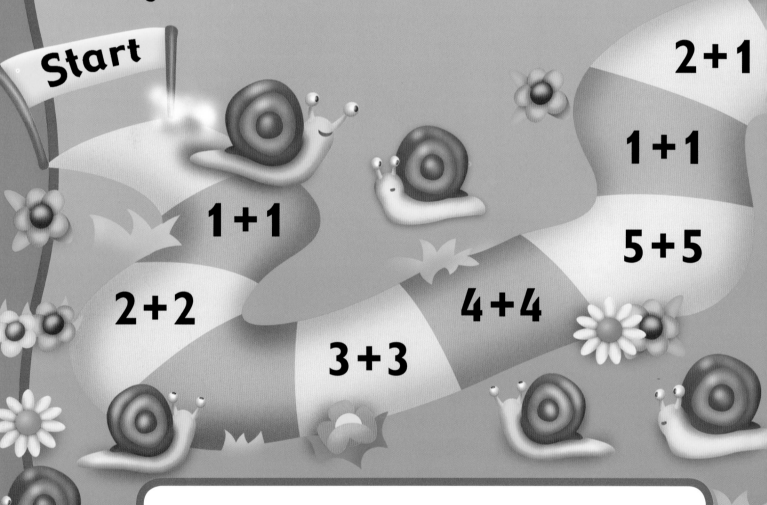

Try these strategies. For doubles, count on in ones like this, 4 and 5, 6, 7, 8. For near doubles, double and add 1 like this, 4+4+1.

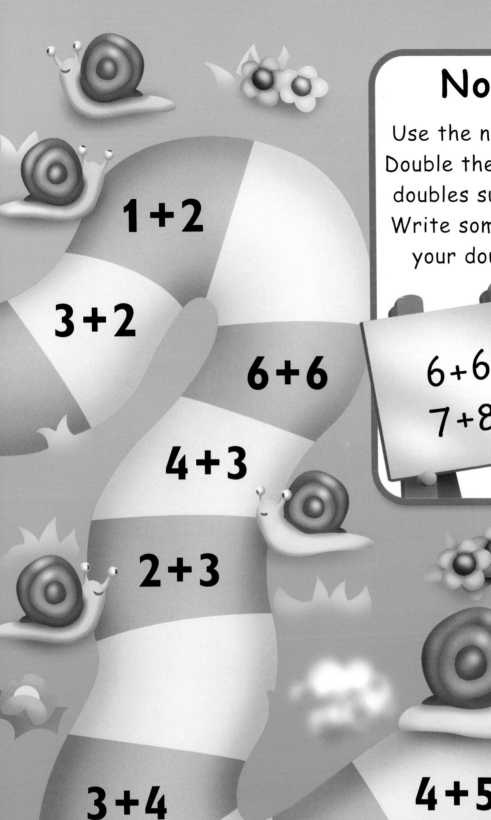

1+2

3+2

6+6

4+3

2+3

3+4

5+4

6+5

4+5

5+6

Finish

Now try this

Use the numbers 6, 7, 8, 9 and 10. Double them. Now can you find near doubles such as 6+7, 7+8 and 8+9? Write some addition sentences for your doubles and near doubles.

6+6=
7+8=

57

Using 5

You will need some counters and a coin. Throw the coin onto the spinner. Split the spinner number into 5 and a bit. So 9 would be 5+4. Now add 5 to 5+4. Cover your answer on one of the stars with a counter.

spinner

6 7
8 9

11

13

12

Throw the coin five more times.
Can you do these additions really quickly now?

12

13

Now try this

Take turns with a friend. Throw the coin onto the spinner twice. Make two '5 and a bit' numbers. Can you see how to add them? The first one to have five correct answers wins!

7+6= 5+2+5+1= 10+3=13

14

14

11

Adding 9 and 11

There is a trick you can use when adding 9. For example, take 6+9. Think of 6+10. Now take away 1. These dogs have some bones. They have hidden 9 more. How many bones has each dog in total?

Suppose the dogs had hidden 11 bones. Try +10 then +1. How many bones has each dog now?

Challenge

The dogs have hidden 8 bones this time. Think about how you could work this out by adding 10. What would you need to take away?

Where have I buried my 8 bones?

Adding teen numbers

Look at the numbers on each tile. Find the total of each pair of tiles. Remember, if you know that 5+4=9 then you can work out that 15+4=19.

Add 1 to each tile. What is the total of each pair now?

Challenge

Write down these addition sentences. 10+4= 11+4= 12+4= Can you work out the answers? What would the next sentence be? And the next one? Tell an adult about the patterns you can see.

An addition problem

Here are some boxes of toys. Each box shows you how many toys are inside. Supposing you wanted 15 toys. Which boxes would you choose?

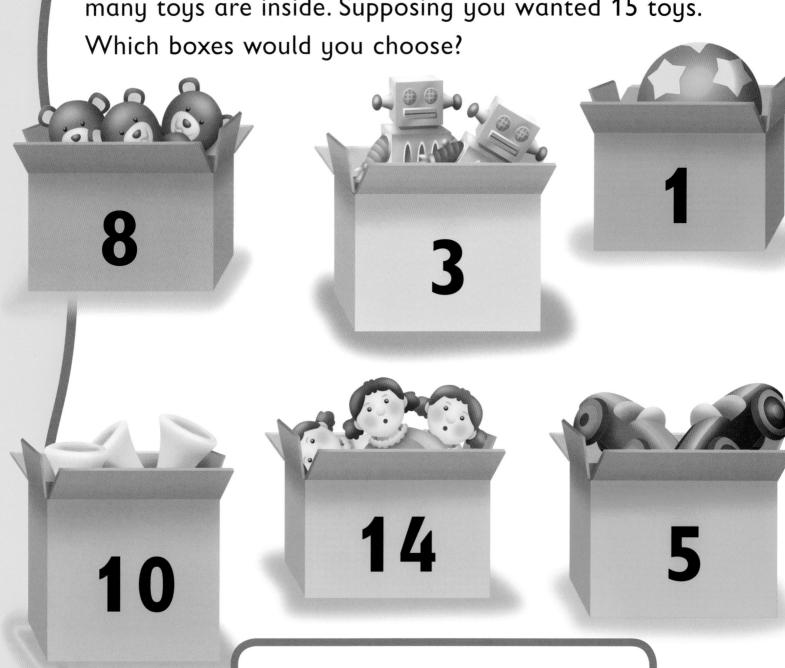

How many different ways can you find to choose 15 toys?

Challenge

Find different ways to choose 20 toys. Write an addition sentence each time.

11+9=20

12

4

6

11

9

7

13

2

65

Subtraction to 5

Each toy box shows you how many toys go inside.
Count how many toys are outside the box.
How many toys are inside the box?

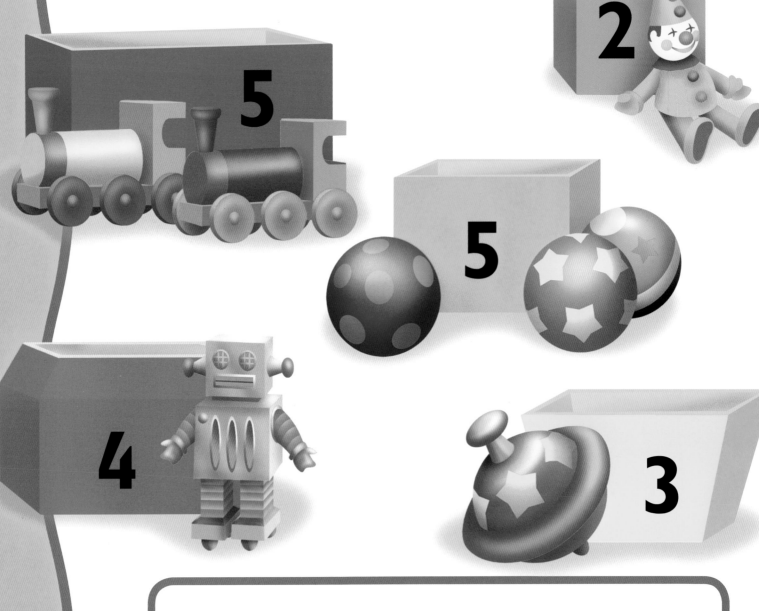

How many boxes have only 1 toy inside?

4

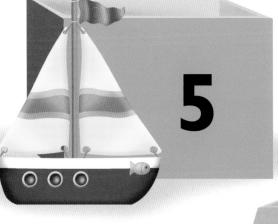

3

Try this

Do this with a friend.
You will need 8 counters and a beaker.
Take turns to hide some of
the counters under the beaker.
Ask your friend to count what is left.
Say, 'How many counters
have I hidden?'

5

4

5

67

Finding differences

The numbers on the bags tell you how many gold pieces should be inside the bags. Say how many. Now count how many gold pieces each pirate has in his hand. So, how many gold pieces are in the bags?

Count up in ones from the lower number to the higher number to find the difference.

Challenge

Do this with a friend.
Take turns to say a number less than 9. The other one works out the difference between that number and 9. Try this again for the difference between a number and 11.

7

The difference between 7 and 9 is 2.

Taking away

Each monkey has some bananas. If you take away 3 bananas, how many will each of them have left?

Try this again. This time, take away 4 bananas.

70

Try this

Take away 5 from 6, 7, 8, 9, 10, 11 and 12. Write a subtraction sentence for each number. Tell someone the patterns that you can see.

$6-5=1$

Subtraction words

Play this game with a friend. You will need a 1–6 dice and two counters. Take turns to throw the dice. Move your counter along the path for the number shown on the dice. Answer the question on the path. If you get the question wrong, move back to where you were before. The first one to reach the *Finish* is the winner.

Start

6–3=

5–1=

What is 3 less than 7?

How much is 2 less than 8?

What is the difference between 10 and 1?

12–8=

10–5=

Take 6 from 7.

What is 7 minus 4?

9–1=

10–0=

With a friend

Take turns to say any number between 0 and 10. The other one says the number that is left when your number is subtracted from 10. See how quickly you can play this game.

9 subtract 2

Say 2 numbers with a difference of 5.

What is 5 taken from 12?

10 subtract 8

How much more is 11 than 7?

Say two numbers with a difference of 3.

How much more is 8 than 3?

What is 10 take away 10?

How many less than 7 is 5?

9–7=

8–5=

Finish

How many more?

Look at one of the boys below. How many toys does he have? How many more toys does he need to make the number on his t-shirt?

Now work out how many more toys the other children need to make the number on their t-shirts.

Challenge

Try this with a friend.
Each of you draw a set of
toys with fewer than 7 in it.
Now swap drawings. Work out how
many more toys are needed to make
a set of 15. Try this 3 more times.

75

Subtraction patterns

Look at the subtraction sentences
that Lenny Lion has written.
Work out what comes next in the
pattern. What would come after that?

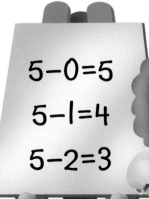

5−0=5
5−1=4
5−2=3

10−0=10
10−1=9

4−0=4
4−1=3

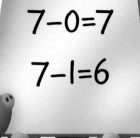

7−0=7
7−1=6

8−0=8
8−1=7

Now try the other patterns.

76

$6 - 0 = 6$

$6 - 1 = 5$

Find out

Look at this number pattern
$12 - 0 = 12$ $12 - 1 = 11$.
Write the pattern so that you finish it.
Explain to an adult what patterns
you can see.

$12 - 0 = 12$

$9 - 0 = 9$

$9 - 1 = 8$

$5 - 0 = 5$

$5 - 1 = 4$

$3 - 0 = 3$

$3 - 1 = 2$

Taking away 9 or 11

There is a trick you can use when taking away 9.
Take 16–9. Think of 16–10. Now add 1. Look at the sheep.
If 9 run away, how many will be left? Take 9 away from
the other sets of animals.

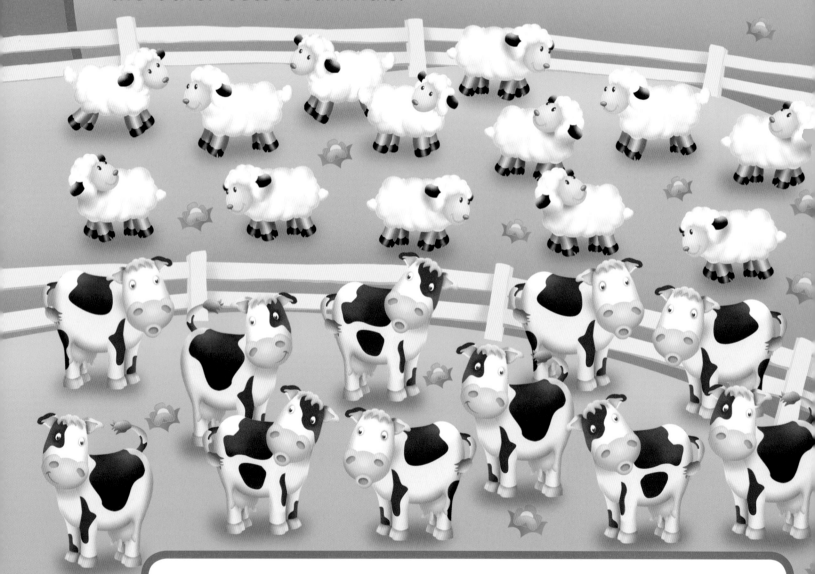

Now suppose 11 animals run away. Try –10 then –1.
How many animals will be left in each set now?

Now try this

Eight animals have run away from each field. Think about how you could work this out by taking away 10. What would you need to add? How many animals are left in each field now?

A subtraction problem

Look at the numbers on the runners.
Find pairs of numbers which have
a difference of 3.

5

2

10

12

1

9

4

6

You may find it helpful to write some subtraction
sentences to remind you of the numbers you have tried.

Challenge

Write 10 pairs of numbers which have a difference of 4. Here is a subtraction sentence to start you off.

10−6=4

11

8

3

7

Finish

I know all this!

You can make an addition sentence for the numbers on the red kite like this: 5+2=7. You can also make 2+5=7. Make two addition sentences for each kite.

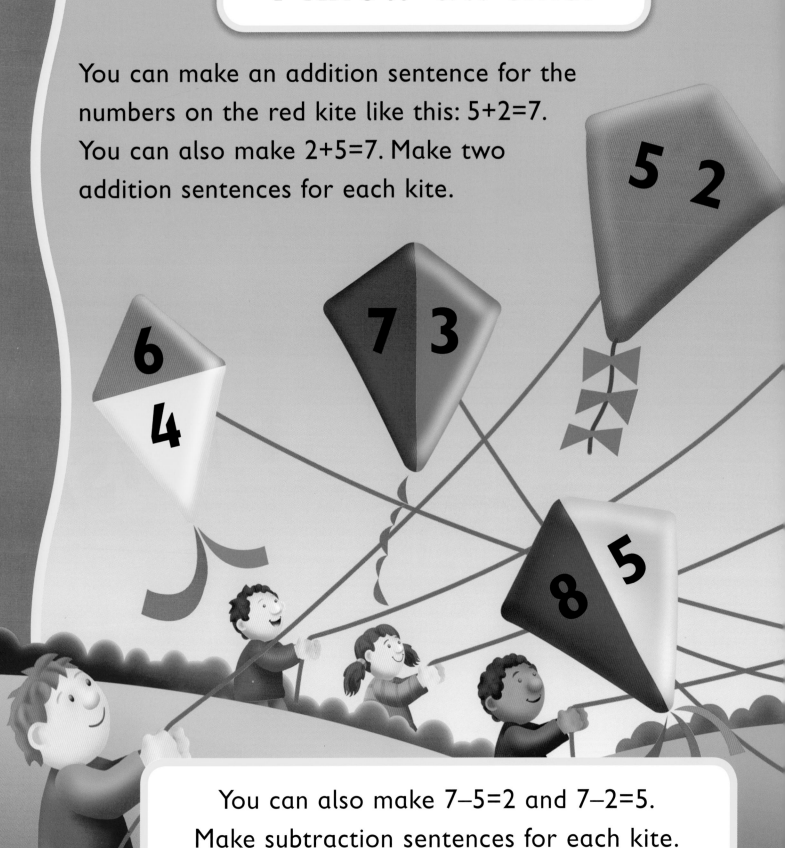

You can also make 7−5=2 and 7−2=5. Make subtraction sentences for each kite.

Now try this

Work with a friend. One of you writes down a number sentence like 6+3=9. The other one writes down the other three number sentences which use the same numbers. Now swap over.

3+6=9
9−3=6
9−6=3

Missing numbers

You need a 1–6 dice, two counters and a friend. Take turns to throw the dice. Move your counter to that number on the path. Now find the missing number in the number sentence. If you are correct, leave your counter where it is. If you are wrong, move your counter back to where you were.

Start

5+3=☐

6+4=☐

7–1=☐

☐+3=9

9–3=☐

☐+2=7

2+☐=6

5+☐=9

What could go in the missing number boxes? Can you make five different number sentences?

□ + □ =8.

Now try this.

12− □ = □

8− □ =6

6− □ =2

6− □ =0

□ −3=4

□ −4=5

□ +5=10

9− □ =2

6− □ =3

Finish

Recognizing coins

Collect together 10 coins. Say their names. How many different sizes are there? How many different colours? Place a coin on each purse shown here.

How much is each coin worth?

Now try this

Which of your coins is worth the least? Which is worth the most? Now put your coins in order of how much they are worth.

Paying at the shops

You will need 10 coins. Decide which shoes you would like to buy and count out the coins into the silver circles. How many coins do you have left?

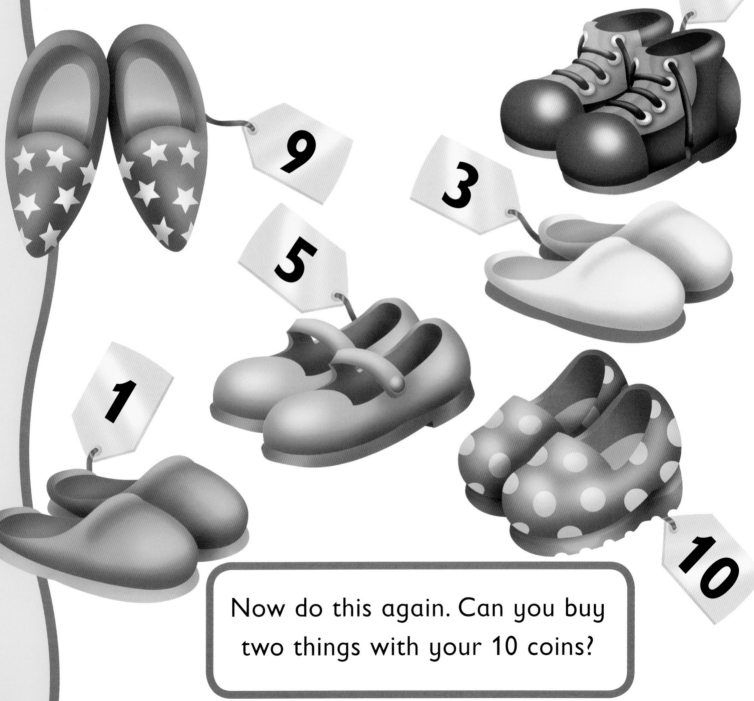

Now do this again. Can you buy two things with your 10 coins?

8

2

6

7

Challenge

Can you find three things to
buy with your 10 coins?
How many different ways
can you do this?

Giving change

Choose something to buy. Pick a coin to use, either the 10 or 20 one below. Work out how much change you will get by counting up from the price.

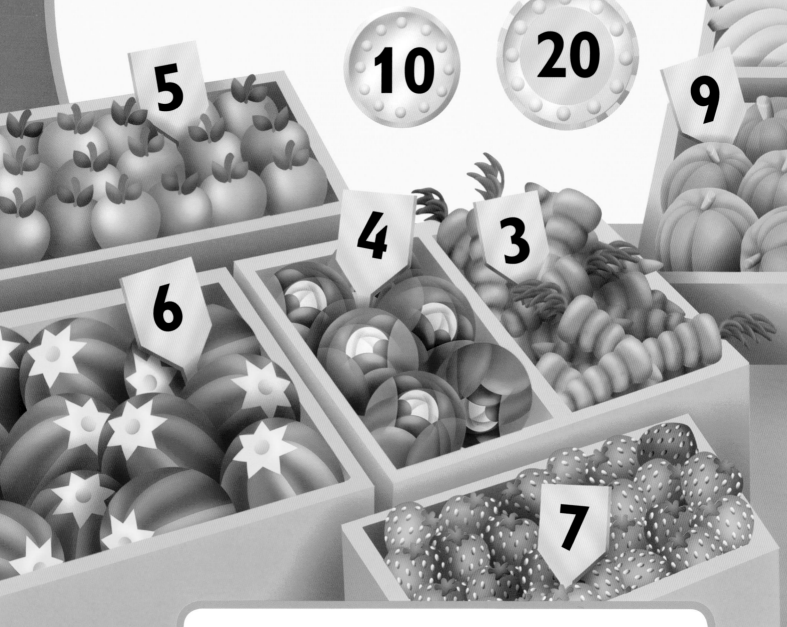

Buy two things this time. Choose a coin.
Work out your change.

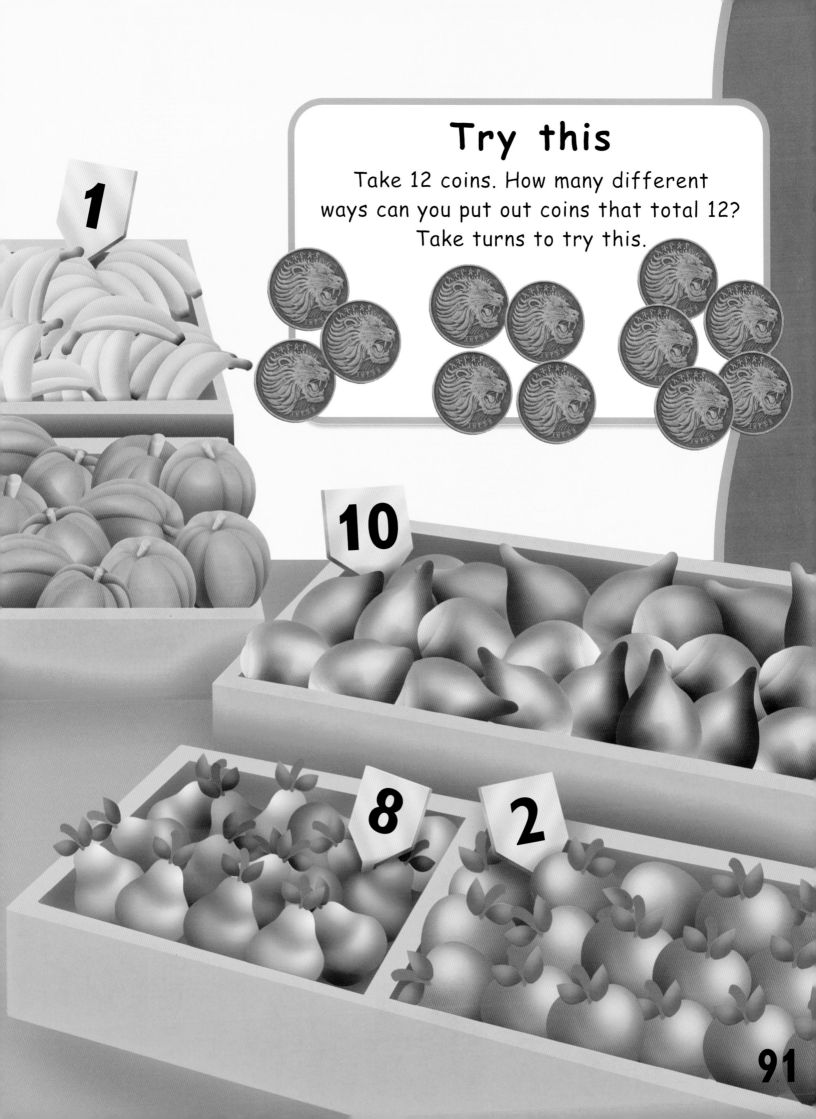

Try this

Take 12 coins. How many different
ways can you put out coins that total 12?
Take turns to try this.

1

10

8

2

Number game

You will need some counters and a friend. Choose two numbers between 1 and 10. Add your numbers together. Put a counter on the person below with the answer. If the number is already covered, you lose that turn. The winner is the one who covers the most people.

Can you find a way to cover every number?

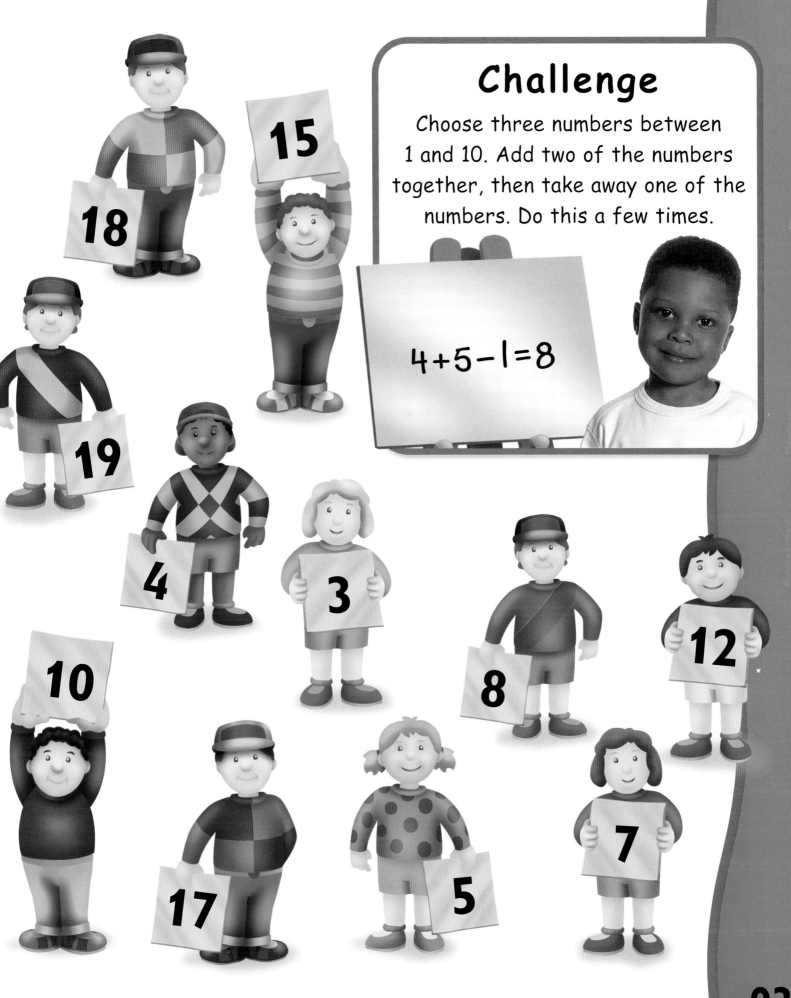

15

18

Challenge

Choose three numbers between 1 and 10. Add two of the numbers together, then take away one of the numbers. Do this a few times.

$4+5-1=8$

19

4

3

8

12

10

17

5

7

93

A wormy problem

Some children measured these worms using buttons. The difference in length between the two worms was four buttons. How long could each worm be?

Now find five more lengths for each worm to be.

Challenge

Suppose the difference in length between the worms is six buttons. Find five lengths that each worm could be.

1 and 7

What's my number?

Read the clues. Find the number on the trophies.

14   **16**   **17**   **18**   **19**

I am larger than 10 but smaller than 18.
I am even.
I am not 14.
What number am I?

I am not even.
I am less than 20 but more than 15.
I am the same as 8+9.
What number am I?

Tell someone how you worked out the answers.

I am even.
I am between
13 and 15.
What number am I?

Try this

With a friend, take turns to think
of a number. Think of some clues.
Say your clues to your friend.
Can they work out your number?

My number
is less than 9.
My number is
not even.

5?

I am not a double.
I am between 15 and 20.
I am not 17.
What number am I?

I am a double.
I am larger than 16.
I am smaller than 20.
What number am I?

Kittens in baskets

You will need 20 counters or coins. These are your kittens. The kittens have been naughty. While their mothers were not looking, they sneaked out of their baskets. Can you put them back? Each basket can have any even number of kittens in it.

Can you find another way to do this?

Can you put the kittens into the baskets so that each basket has an odd number of kittens? Find another way to do this.

Adding small numbers

Add each set of numbers on the cars. Find that total on a driver's helmet. That's the driver of that car!

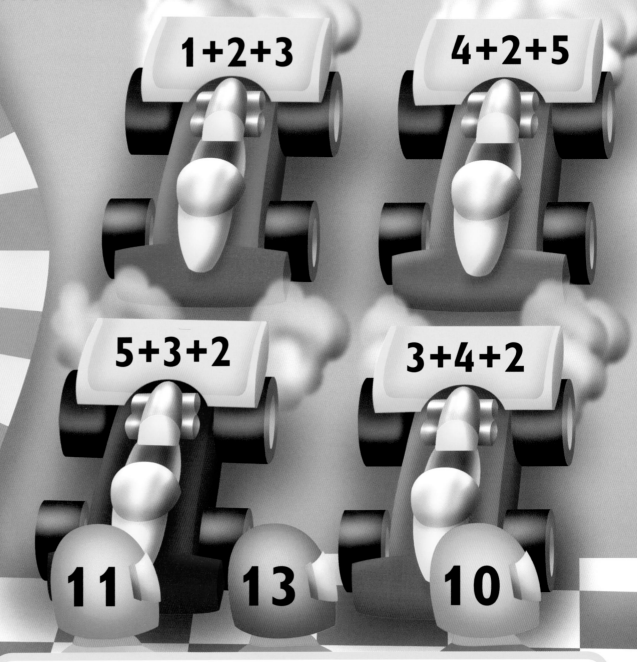

1+2+3

4+2+5

5+3+2

3+4+2

11

13

10

What happens if you add the numbers in a different order? Is the total the same or different?

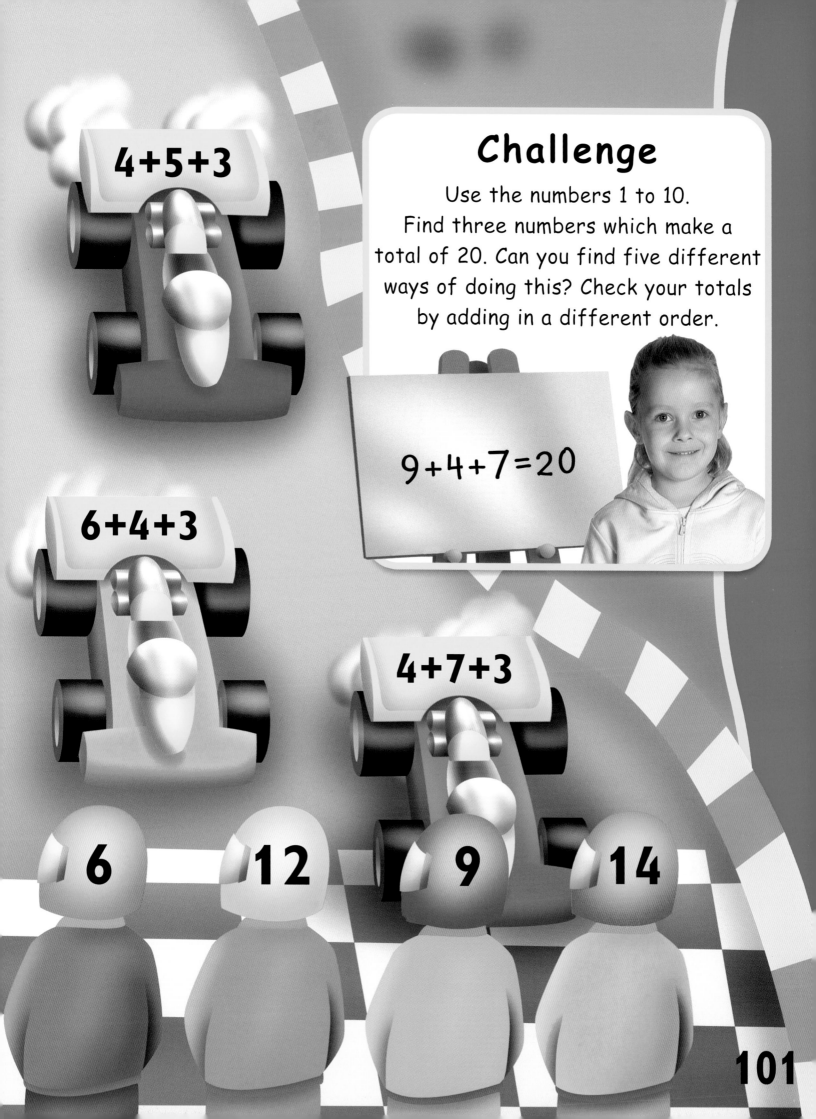

4+5+3

6+4+3

4+7+3

Challenge

Use the numbers 1 to 10.
Find three numbers which make a
total of 20. Can you find five different
ways of doing this? Check your totals
by adding in a different order.

9+4+7=20

6   12   9   14

I know these

You will need a friend, a coin and two counters. Take turns to throw the coin onto the spinner. Move your counter forward the number your coin lands on, and answer the question on the lily pad. If you answer correctly, leave your counter there. If you are wrong, move back to where you were. The winner is the first one to the finish.

Start

5+4

3+6

50+50

4+2

5+3

30+70

5+5

7−2

8−3

5−3

8−7

10−10

100−80

4+6

10+90

102

spinner

1 2
4 3

Now try this

Use three of these numbers: 1, 2, 3, 4, 5, 6, 7. You can only choose each number once for each addition sentence you come up with. Write 4 different addition sentences with the total of 10.

$3+6+1=10$

100–30

100–60

8+2

9+1

20+80

2+8

10–5

3+7

20+8

40+60

100–50

9–3

6–6

6+2

Finish

1+9

100–100

103

I know totals for 20

You will need 21 counters or coins. Choose two numbers from the animals that total 20. Cover your numbers with the counters.

Find different ways to make a total of 20. Can you cover 20 of the numbers?

Challenge

Look at the numbers on the animals. Add two numbers together to make a total of 30. Can you find five ways of doing this?

?+?=30

Tens and units

Help the post carriers work out how many letters to put into their bags by finding the answer to the number sentences on their postbags. An easy way to work this out is to add or subtract the tens first, then do the units.

92–51

31+47

67–13

23+41

48–15

Which bag will have the most letters in it?
Which bag will have the fewest letters in it?

64+23

43+36

76−23

85−62

44+32

54−24

Try this

Choose a number from here:
20, 30, 40, 50, 60.
Now choose a number from here:
15, 17, 23, 26, 38.
Add the two numbers together.
In the answer, what do you notice
about the tens and the units digits?
Try this four more times.

20+15=

Finding small differences

Find a butterfly with the same number difference as the orange one. Count up from the smaller to the larger number to find the difference.

Find the other pairs of butterflies with the same difference.

62 – 54

45 – 39

81 – 78

61 – 57

73 – 67

51 – 46

Challenge

Use two-digit numbers.
Find five pairs of numbers
with a difference of 6.
Write your pairs of numbers down.

64–58=6

Four in a row

You will need some counters. Choose two numbers from the animal statues below. Decide whether to add or find the difference between your numbers. If your answer is on the grid, cover that number with a counter. Try to make a line of four counters from your answers.

Play the game with a friend. The first one to get four in a row wins!

Try this

Make your own four in a row game. Write some numbers that can be added or subtracted. Write the answers in a grid. Write some more numbers until the grid is full. Now ask your friend to try to make four in a row.

72 36

9

10

13

53

56

69

49

Seaside shopping

You will need some coins. Pretend to buy two of the things below. Give the correct amount of money in change.

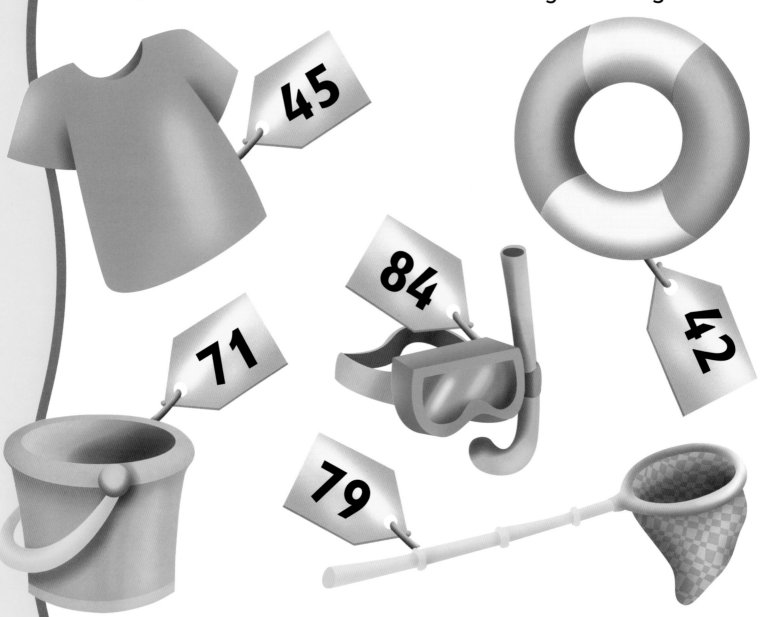

Now try this again. This time, give too much money when you pay. Work out the correct change.

37

Find out

Look in a magazine or, with adult supervision, use the Internet. How much are your favourite CDs? Which two CDs would you like to buy? How much would that cost in total?

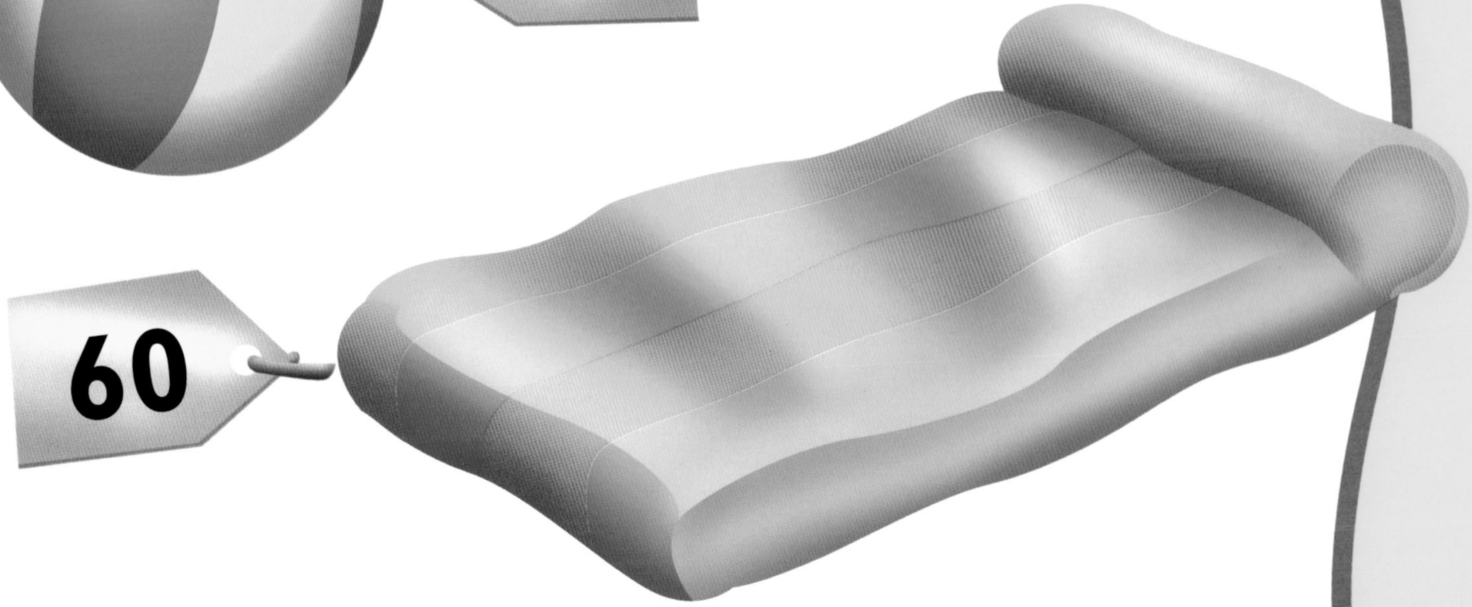

25

58

99

60

113

Supporting notes for adults

Counting on – pages 48–49

Putting the larger set first and counting on for the second set is a very useful mental strategy. Ask the children to count on in ones. They may find it helpful to keep a check by using their fingers, so that they count on for the correct amount. For example, 6+3 is 6 and 7, 8, 9. The children put up three fingers, one at a time, to keep a check of their count.

Adding small numbers – pages 50–51

Encourage the children to count on in ones from the larger number. For example, for 5+6 say 6 and 7, 8, 9, 10, 11. So 5+6 is 11. The children can keep track of the mental count using their fingers. Encourage the children to write an addition sentence using + and =.

Totals of 10 – pages 52–53

The children will find it helpful to use their fingers at first. Say, 'I'll say a number. You show me with your fingers how many more I will need to make 10'. The children can then use their 10 digits to find the answer.

Adding to 10 – pages 54–55

The children will need to have rapid recall of all addition facts to at least 5+5, and then begin to know all addition facts to 10+10. Encourage them to use strategies, such as 'Put the larger number in your head and count on in ones', where they do not have rapid recall of the fact.

Doubles and near doubles – pages 56–57

The children will find the strategy of counting on from one of the numbers helpful. Where it is a near double, suggest that they count on from the smaller number and add 1. Some children may prefer to count on from the larger number and subtract 1. This is also a good strategy.

Using 5 – pages 58–59

Discuss the partitioning strategy with the children. Take 5+8. This is the same as 5+5+3 or 10+3. If the children are beginning to understand about place value, then they will not need to add the 3 to the 10, instead they will see that 10+3=13, because the '3' moves directly to the units place.

Adding 9 and 11 — pages 60–61

Understanding place value will help the children to see that if 10 is added to any number, then it leaves the units unchanged. For example, 6+10 is 16. If the children are unsure, use a number line at first so that they can count on 10, then add/subtract 1 to complete the calculation.

Adding teen numbers — pages 62–63

Encourage the children to use what they already know, or can calculate mentally, in order to work out what they do not know. If the children are unclear about moving from, for example, 5+3=8 to 15+3=18, then use a number line and show them how this is the same as 10+5+3.

An addition problem – pages 64–65

The children may find it helpful to write the numbers on the boxes of toys onto some pieces of paper. Then ask them to try different combinations of their boxes of toys to find totals of 15. Some children may find a number line from 0 to 20 useful as an aid to calculating. They can count along the line. However, do encourage mental counting in order to find totals.

Subtraction to 5 – pages 66–67

If the children do not yet know these subtraction facts, they will find it helpful to count on their fingers to find the answers, then to count along a number line. Encourage them next to count along a mental number line 'in their heads'.

Finding differences — pages 68–69

Begin by counting up from the lower to the higher number, keeping a track of how many on fingers. For example, for the difference between 4 and 7 count: 5, 6, 7. This gives a count of 3, which is the difference. With practice, the children will begin to make the count mentally.

Taking away – pages 70–71

Encourage the children to explain which strategy they used to take away.
Some may still count on their fingers. If so, provide a 0 to 10 number line and
use this to count on from the lower to the higher number. The children can keep a tally
with their fingers. Progress to using a mental number line for
counting on, where the children do not have recall of the answer.

Subtraction words – pages 72–73

This activity gives children practice in using subtraction vocabulary.
Read the questions together. If the children do not have rapid recall of the answer,
discuss how the answer could be found, such as counting up from the lower to the
higher number, at first on fingers and then, when confident, along a mental number line.

How many more? – pages 74–75

Encourage the children to count up in ones from the lower to the higher number.
Encourage them to do this mentally. At first, they may need to keep track of the count by
using their fingers. For the numbers 3 and 8 say, '4, 5, 6, 7, 8. So that is 5 that we counted.
So we need 5 more than 3 to make 8.'

Subtraction patterns – pages 76–77

If children know a subtraction fact, then they can work out a closely related fact.
For example, if they know 8–1=7, then they can work out that 8–2 is 6, or 1 less than
before because 2 is 1 more than 1. Encourage them to use this as a mental strategy.
They will find it useful at first to write out the sequence of subtraction sentences.

Taking away 9 or 11 – pages 78–79

The children will need to understand that if 10 is subtracted from any number, then it leaves
the units unchanged. For example, 16–10 is 6. If children are unsure, at first use a number
line so that they can count back 10, then add/subtract 1 to complete the calculation.

A subtraction problem – pages 80–81

Encourage the children to talk about which strategy they used to find the
pairs with a difference of 3. Some may count on 3 from any of the numbers and look
to see if the number they reach is there. Suggest that they begin with the smallest number,
then the next smallest, and so on, so they work systematically.

I know all this! – pages 82–83

If children know, or can rapidly recall, one addition or subtraction fact, then
they can deduce three other facts. If children are unsure about this, write down one
of the facts like this: 6+3=9. Then ask, 'What is 3+6? What do you notice? So what is 9–3?
And 9–6? Now what do you notice?' If children find the calculation difficult,
count together, using a mental or real number line.

Missing numbers – pages 84–85

If children are unsure how to find what is missing for 2+☐=6, discuss how they can
count on from 2, in ones, to 6. Then ask, 'Is this true, 2+4=6?' For subtraction, try
counting up like this: for 9–☐=2, count on from the 2 to the 9. Ask, 'Is this true 9–7=2?'

Recognizing coins – pages 86–87

Encourage children to sort real coins and to name them. Separate the coins
by their colour, so that all the brass/copper/silver coins are together. Discuss how to
recognize each coin by size and color and by the designs on the coins.

Paying at the shops – pages 88–89

Use the lowest value coins in your currency. Encourage the children to count the coins out, one at a time, until they have enough for their purchase. Where they are 'buying' two items, encourage them to total the two amounts mentally, by counting on, then they can count out the correct number of coins.

Giving change – pages 90–91

Help children to understand the method of giving change by counting up. Explain that you need to count up from the price to the amount of money that you give, like this: 'and 5, 6, 7, 8, 9, 10. I counted 6, so the change is 6.'

Number game – pages 92–93

This game encourages children to total pairs of numbers mentally. If children find this hard, discuss the strategies they could use, such as doubling, near doubles (double and add one) and counting on in ones from the larger number.

A wormy problem – pages 94–95

This problem is about the difference between pairs of numbers. If the children find this difficult, begin with the number 1 and ask, 'What number would be 4 more than 1? Yes, 5. So the difference between 5 and 1 is 4.' Then try 4 more than 2, so that the children begin to see a pattern forming of 1, 5; 2, 6; 3, 7 and so forth.

What's my number? – pages 96–97

Read the clues together. Discuss each one and ask 'What does it tell you?' If children are unsure about odd and even numbers, count from 0 to 20 in twos and agree that these are the even numbers. Now do the same for counting in twos starting on 1, and agree that these are the odd numbers.

Kittens in baskets – pages 98–99

Children will explore adding four small even numbers to make 20. Begin by counting in twos from 0 to 20 to remind the children of the even numbers. There are many different ways to put the kittens back in their baskets. For example: 4, 6, 4, 6; 8, 2, 8, 2; 2, 4, 6, 8 and so forth. Odd numbers are possible, too: 5, 5, 5, 5; 9, 1, 9, 1 and so on. If the original puzzle is too hard, begin with 10 counters, so that the kittens could go into their baskets like this: 2, 2, 2, 4. This is the only solution. Now try 20 kittens.

Adding small numbers – pages 100–101

If the children need further help, there are two strategies that they might find useful: finding pairs of numbers which make 10, then adding on the third number, such as 4+7+6=4+6+7=10+7=17. Or, putting the largest number first, such as 3+5+4=5+4+3=9+3=12.

I know these – pages 102–103

Encourage the children to answer these questions as quickly as they can. These are addition and subtraction within a total of 10, and addition of decade numbers to 100. If children are unsure, remind them of strategies that they already know, such as counting on from the larger number, and using what they know about single-digit totals to 10 to find decade totals up to 100.

I know totals for 20 – pages 104–105

Knowing totals for 20 is an extension of knowing totals for 10.
For example, 2+8=10 and 12+8=20. If children are unsure, cover over the teen digit and
ask the children to total the units to make totals of 10, then uncover the teen digit to make a
total of 20. Encourage the children to spot the pattern: 0+20=20; 1+19=20; 2+18=20…

Tens and units – pages 106–107

Where the addition or subtraction of the units does not cross the tens barrier, the children can use what
they already know to work out the answer. They will probably find it easier to begin with the tens digits,
then deal with the units. If they are unsure, use a number line and start with the tens digits.

Finding small differences – pages 108–109

Counting up from the smaller to the larger number is a useful strategy when finding small differences.
If children are unsure, use a number line. Start at the smaller number and count up in ones.
The children can keep track of how many are counted on their fingers.
Encourage them to move to doing this mentally.

Four in a row – pages 110–111

This game challenges children to use addition or subtraction facts that they know, or can calculate
mentally. They may find it helpful to have paper and pencil handy when playing this game,
so that they can jot down which numbers they have tried and the totals or differences.

Seaside shopping – pages 112–113

Children will find it useful to have real coins for this activity.
If they find the totalling difficult, they can begin with a selection of coins and
count out what they need for each price, then total the coins. Encourage them
to total mentally, then count out the coins, using the fewest coins possible.

118

Multiplying and dividing

30÷2

50x2

15x2

40÷2

More odds and evens

Play this game with a friend. You will each need a counter. Take turns to toss a third counter onto the spinner below. Move your counter to the first odd or even number. Now it's your friend's turn. Keep doing this, moving to the next odd or even number each time. The first one to 30 wins.

Take turns to point to a number on the track. Say if it is odd or even.

20 **21** **22** **23** **24** **25** **16** **17** **18** **19**

26 **27** **28** **29** **30**

Now try this

Play the game again.
This time take turns to roll
a 1–6 dice. Move your counter
the number of spaces you throw.
Tell your friend whether the
number you land on is odd or even.

Spinner

Even Odd Odd Even

Finish

121

2s, 3s, 4s, 5s and 10s

You will need red and blue counters. Count along the flowerpots in 2s. Put a red counter on each number you land on. Now count along in 4s and use blue counters. Which numbers have both blue and red counters? What can you say about these numbers?

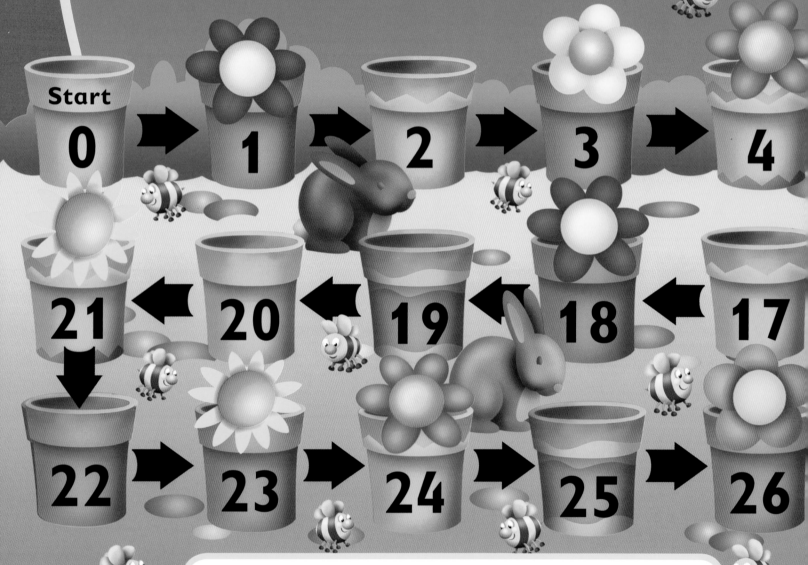

Do this again for counting in 2s and 3s.

Challenge

Which is the first number that comes when you count in 2s and 3s? Yes, it's 6. Now which is the first number that comes when you count in 2s, 3s, 4s and 5s? You may find it helpful to use a number line.

| 0 | 1 | 2 | 3 | 4 |

5 ➡ 6 ➡ 7 ➡ 8 ➡ 9 ➡ 10

16 ⬅ 15 ⬅ 14 ⬅ 13 ⬅ 12 ⬅ 11

27 ➡ 28 ➡ 29 ➡ 30 ➡ **Finish** 31

Using arrays

The bees have arranged the cells for their honey in arrays. Look at the array with 8 squares. It is 4 multiplied by 2, or 4x2. It can also be seen as 2x4. Look at the other arrays. Write a multiplication for each array.

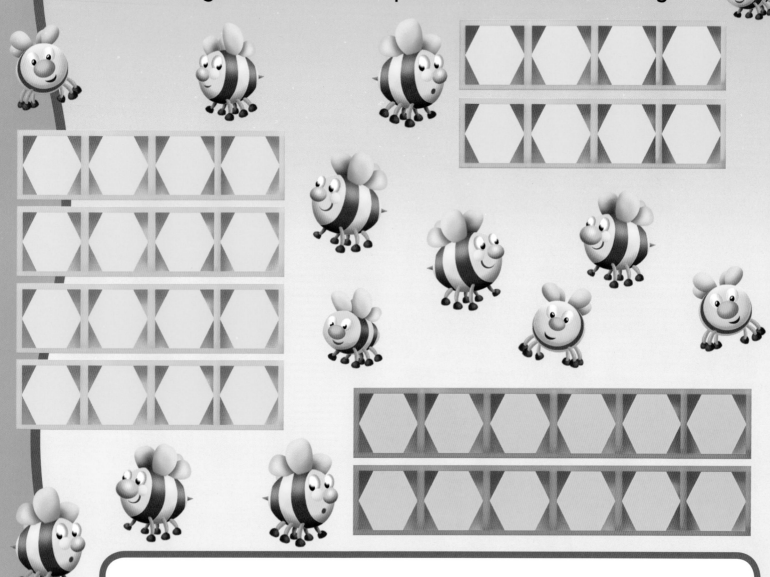

Can you write another multiplication for each array?
Write how many cells there are in each array.

Now try this

Draw an array.
Write 2 multiplications for it.
Do this 5 times.

3×2   2×3

125

Doubling

You will need some counters. Choose a number on the sunken boat. Double it. Can you now find the doubled number? If so, cover both numbers with your counters. If you can't find the double, don't cover any number.

1	26	24	8
12	10	11	30
3	7	28	5

Can you find a way to cover all the numbers on the grid?

126

Find out

Investigate doubling numbers from 16 to 30. Write down the doubles of these numbers. Tell a friend how you worked out these doubles.

Double 16 is 32.

Double 17 is 34.

4	13	22	2
15	16	6	14
18	20	9	

Multiplying by 2s and 10s

Read the multiplication on the card that the boy with blond hair is holding. Find the answer on a card that a girl is holding.

Now match the other multiplications to their answers. Which multiplication sentences have an odd answer?

8x2

10

4x10

40

16

7x2

9x2

6

100

70

Now try this

Think about all the answers to the questions from the 2 times table. Is the answer each time odd or even? Is the answer each time in the 10 times table odd or even? Can you think of a reason for your answers here?

6x2=12
3x10=30

Multiplication for 5s

The bees below are in groups of 5. How many groups are there? So how many bees are there altogether? Now look at the butterflies. They are also in groups of 5. Count the groups. How many butterflies are there altogether?

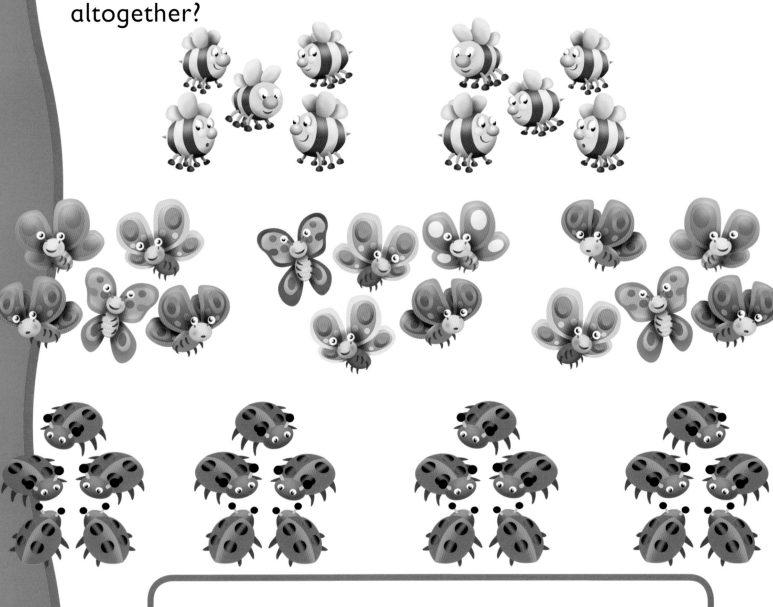

Try this for the other groups of bugs.

Now try this

Draw your own groups of bugs to show 9x5 and 10x5. Write how many in total there are each time.

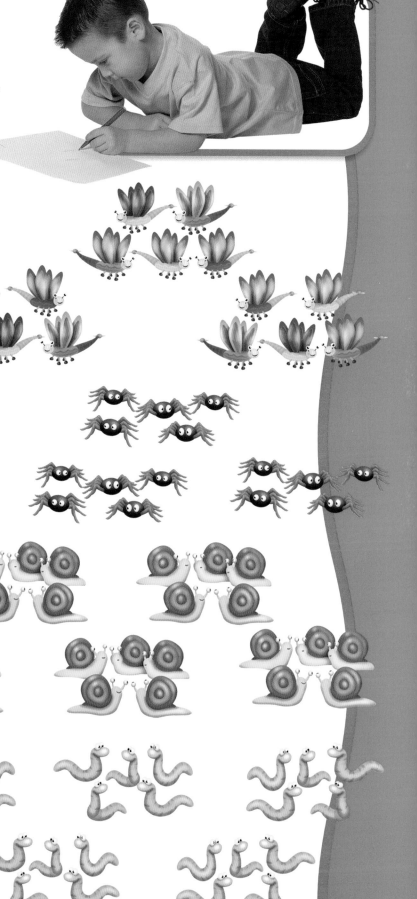

More doubles

The wind has blown away the answers to the double questions the animals are holding. Help the animals to find the answers.

Which of these doubles are also a multiple of 10?
How can you tell?

80

30

25x2

20x2

100

50

35x2

45x2

Try this

Take turns to write down a number which is in the count of 5s, such as 5, 10, 15. Ask your friend to say its double. See how quickly you can do ten of these.

Double 15 is 30.

15

Number sort

Read the labels on the bags and decide where each number on the right should go. Some numbers can go into more than one bag.

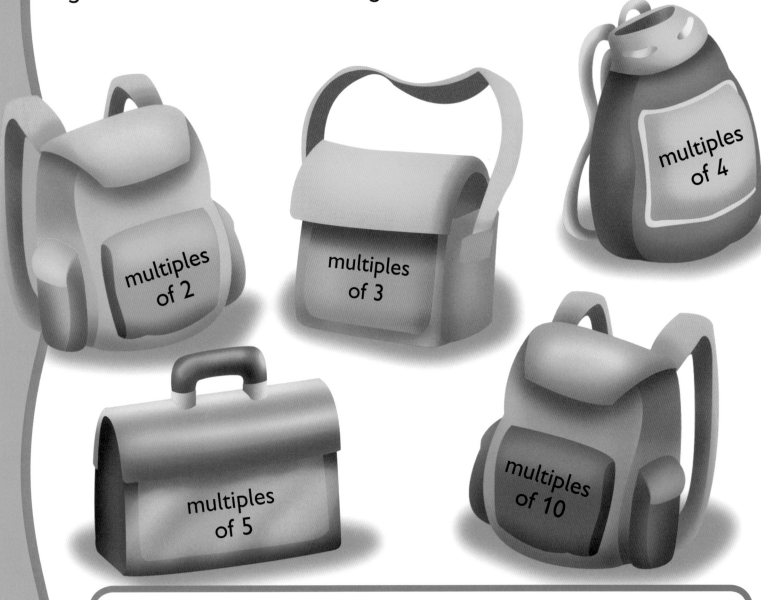

One of the numbers will not fit into any of the bags. Can you find it?

6

32

27

12

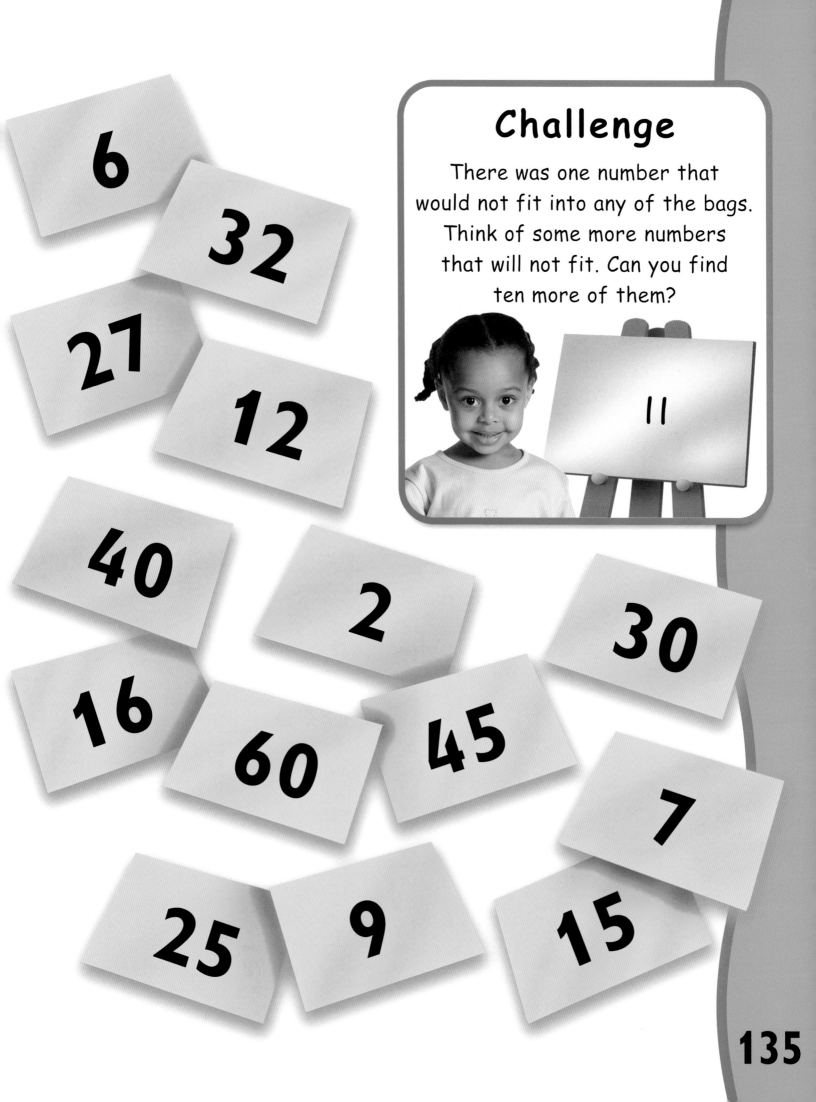

Challenge

There was one number that would not fit into any of the bags. Think of some more numbers that will not fit. Can you find ten more of them?

11

40

2

30

16

60

45

7

25

9

15

How many vehicles?

Look at all the car and bicycle wheels below.
How many cars do the wheels belong to?
How many bicycles do the wheels belong to?

Talk about how you worked out the answer.

Challenge

Look again at the picture. Some cars have only three wheels. How many three-wheeled cars could there be?

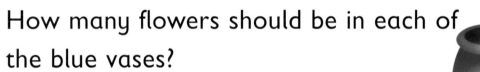

Equal grouping

Count the orange flowers. Now count the blue vases.
The flowers must be grouped equally into each vase.
How many flowers should be in each of
the blue vases?

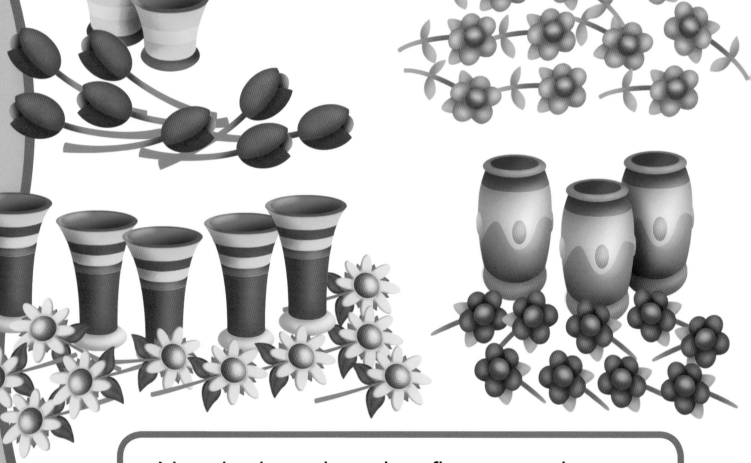

Now look at the other flowers and vases.
How many flowers should be grouped
equally in each vase?

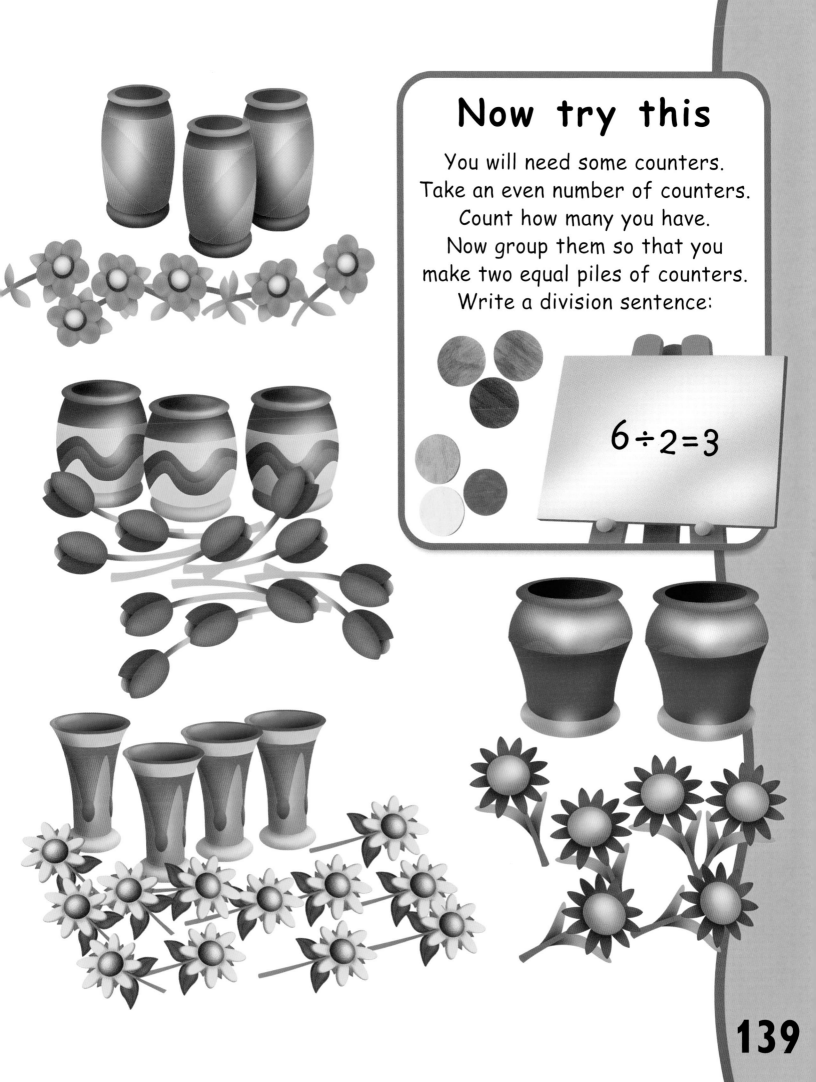

Now try this

You will need some counters.
Take an even number of counters.
Count how many you have.
Now group them so that you
make two equal piles of counters.
Write a division sentence:

$$6 \div 2 = 3$$

Equal sharing

Count the bones. Then count the dogs. Finally, share the bones equally between the dogs. Each dog must have the same number of bones.

Try this again with the other animals and things to share.

Challenge

You will need 20 counters, paper and a pencil. Draw two large circles. Can you share the 20 counters evenly between the circles? Now try again for 3, 4, 5, and 10 circles. Which number of circles leaves some counters left over?

Dividing by 2

You can use what you know about multiplying by 2 to help you to divide by 2, so 5x2=10 then 10÷2=5.

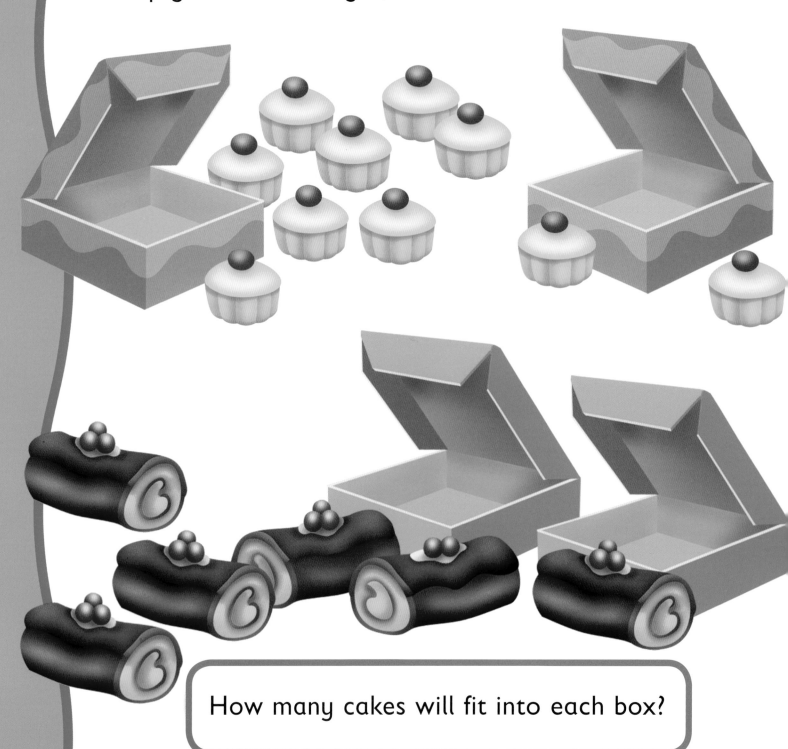

How many cakes will fit into each box?

Now try this

Write out all the multiplication facts for the 2 times table like this: 1x2=2 2x2=4. Now write out the division facts for 2 like this: 2÷2=1 4÷2=2. Compare your two lists. What do you notice?

1x2=2
2x2=4
3x2=6

2÷2=1
4÷2=2
6÷2=3

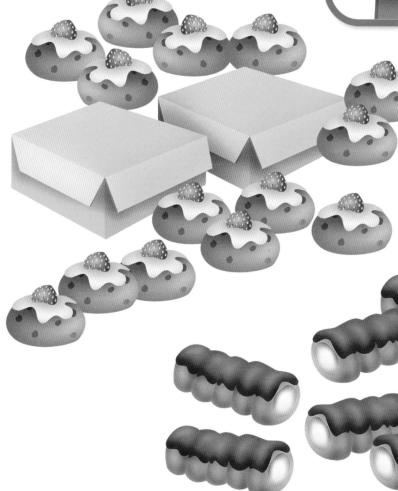

Dividing by 10

Do this with a friend. You will each need some counters. Take turns to throw a counter onto the runway. Divide the number that your counter lands on by 10. Find the correct answer on the lorries and put a counter on it. The winner is the one with more counters on the lorries, when all 10 numbers are covered.

Use what you know about multiplying by 10 to help you to divide by 10, so 5x10=50 and 50÷10=5.

With a friend

Write down all the division facts for 10 in order: 10÷10=1 and so on. Now take turns to say a multiplication fact that goes with each division fact, such as 1 multiplied by 10 equals 10.

$$10 \div 10 = 1$$
$$1 \times 10 = 10$$

40 50

90 100

1 2 3 4 5

6 7 8 9 10

Dividing by 3, 4 and 5

Find out the number of each runner. Work out the answer to the division sentence on the runners' shirts. Find their missing number on the water bottles.

12÷3

20÷4

15÷5

10÷5

18÷3

24÷3

Which division sentences have an even answer?
Which division sentences have an odd answer?

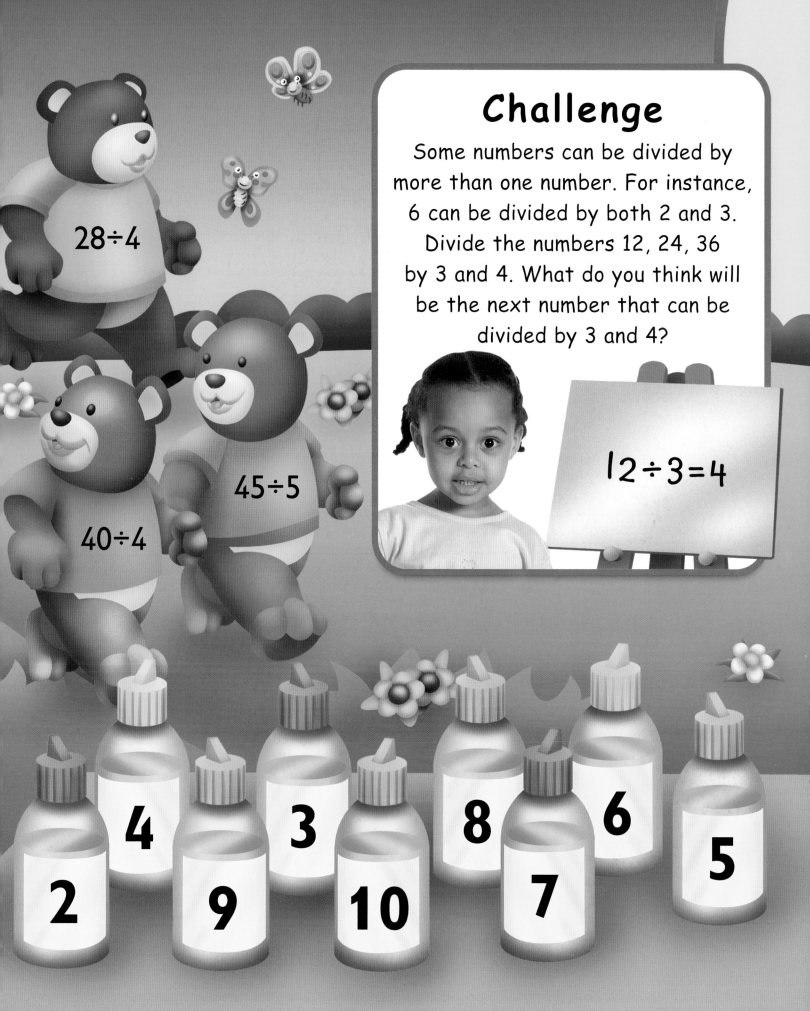

28÷4

40÷4

45÷5

Challenge

Some numbers can be divided by more than one number. For instance, 6 can be divided by both 2 and 3. Divide the numbers 12, 24, 36 by 3 and 4. What do you think will be the next number that can be divided by 3 and 4?

$12 \div 3 = 4$

2   4   9   3   10   8   7   6   5

Finding remainders

Count the rabbits. Put the rabbits into the two hutches so that each hutch has the same number of rabbits. Sometimes when we divide, it is not possible to do this exactly. There is a remainder, or something left over. How many rabbits are left over?

Now try this with the other animals and their homes. Find the remainders.

Challenge

Which numbers will divide into 30 without leaving a remainder? Try dividing by 2, 3, 4, 5 and 10.

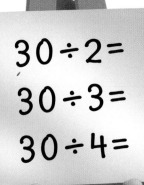

$$30 \div 2 =$$
$$30 \div 3 =$$
$$30 \div 4 =$$

Halves and quarters

Help the children to share out the fruit. They would like to have half each.

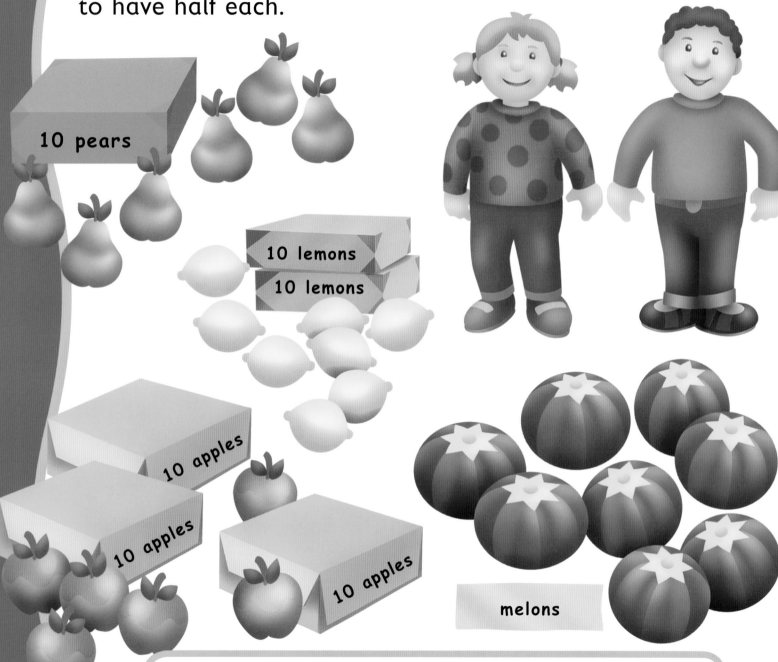

10 pears

10 lemons

10 lemons

10 apples

10 apples

10 apples

10 apples

melons

Now two friends have joined the children. Give each child one quarter each of the fruit.

tomatoes

bananas

strawberries

Now try this

You will need some squared paper and coloured pencils. Draw a rectangle. Colour half the squares blue. Draw different rectangles and colour half blue. Try colouring in different ways.

10 oranges

10 oranges

151

Finding halves

All the numbers on the clowns' balloons are halves of the numbers on the elephants. Match each number on an elephant to its half on a clown's balloon.

Some of the elephant numbers can be divided into quarters. Can you find two of these?

9

90

Challenge

Which of these numbers can be quartered: 4, 14, 24, 34? Write down five more numbers that can be quartered.

$4 \div 4 =$

7

16

6

8

70

12

153

Fingers and thumbs

Some of the children in Mrs Jones' class counted their fingers and thumbs and discovered that there were 90 in total. How many children were there? If some children counted fingers, thumbs and toes and counted to 100, how many children is that?

Tell a friend how you worked out the answer.

Challenge

How many children are in your class at school? How many fingers and thumbs are there altogether? How many toes? So, how many digits (fingers, thumbs and toes) are there in total in your class?

Supporting notes for adults

More odds and evens – pages 120–121

Count in 2s, from 0 to about 30, and say that these are the even numbers. Repeat this, but start on 1, and explain that these are the odd numbers. Children can count, jumping with their fingers along the pathway, to point to the odd or even numbers.

2s, 3s, 4s, 5s and 10s – pages 122–123

If children count correctly along the flowerpots, they will discover that certain numbers appear in counts of 2s and 4s, for example, 4, 8 and 12. They will also begin to see that the numbers that come in counts of 2s and 5s, are the decade numbers, as well as the numbers that come in counts of 10s. Similarly, by comparing counts of 2s and 3s, they will find the multiples of 6: 6, 12, 18... The *Challenge* answer is 60.

Using arrays – pages 124–125

An array is a rectangle which shows multiplication. Each array can be read in two ways, for example, 3x4 and 4x3. If children are unsure about this, help them to make their own rectangular arrays and ask them to count along one side, then along the adjoining side, so that they find the multiplication numbers. They can count all the cells to find the multiplication, for example, 4x3=12.

Doubling – pages 126–127

If children are unsure about the doubles of numbers to 15, then use some counters. Count out, say, 12, then another 12, match them to show that there are 2 sets of 12. Now ask the children to count on from 12: 13, 14, 15... 24 and agree that double 12 is 24.

Multiplying by 2s and 10s – pages 128–129

Children need to have rapid recall of the multiplication facts for the 2 and 10 times tables. If they are unsure about an answer, try counting in 2s or 10s, keeping a tally with fingers of how many 2s or 10s have been counted, until the required point in the count has been reached. For example, for 4x2 count 2, 4, 6, 8. So 4x2 is 8.

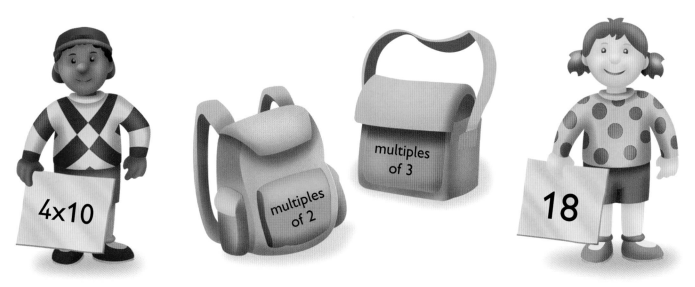

Multiplication for 5s – pages 130–131

Discourage children from counting each insect one by one. The activity is designed so that they should count in 5s: 5, 10, 15, 20… If the children are unsure about this, then count together in 5s. You may want to practice the count before starting the activity on the page.

More doubles – pages 132–133

This extends children's understanding of doubles to doubles of numbers in the 5 times table. If children are unsure, count up from 0 in 5s to reach the start number. Ask, 'How many fives is that? Now count on for the same number of 5s.' For example, to find double 20: 5, 10, 15, 20. That is 4 lots of 5. So 25, 30, 35, 40 gives another 4 lots of 5 to reach 40, or double 20.

Number sort – pages 134–135

If the children need more help with this activity, use the *2s, 3s, 4s, 5s and 10s* activity on pages 122 and 123. Now ask for each number on this page, 'Is it a multiple of 2? How can you tell? Is it a multiple of 3… 4… ?' Children may find it helpful to count in 2s, 3s, 4s… to check. The odd one out is 7, which is a prime number. Some numbers, such as 16 and 32 (multiples of 2 and 4) and 6 (multiple of 2 and 3) could go into either of the bags.

How many vehicles? – pages 136–137

The children need to count all the car wheels, then all the bicycle wheels. Suggest that they jot down on paper their totals. In order to work out how many cars there are, they may find it helpful to count in 4s, and keep a tally on their fingers, until they reach the total of wheels for the cars. Similarly, for the bicycles, they can count in 2s.

Equal grouping – pages 138–139

If the children are unsure about division by repeated subtraction, or grouping, provide some counters. Ask the children to count out the same quantity of counters as there are flowers, then to divide the counters between the vases equally. They can count each set of counters to check that each vase has the same quantity.

Equal sharing – pages 140–141

Children may begin to share by saying, 'one for you and one for me', until they have shared all the items. Encourage them to think about the multiplication facts that they know. For example, if they know that 3x2=6, then 6 shared by 3 is 2.

Dividing by 2 – pages 142–143

Children should begin to derive the division facts for 2 from their knowledge of the 2 times table. Say together the 2s multiplication table, then say the division table: 2 divided by 2 is 1; 4 divided by 2 is 2… If they are still unsure, then start with some counters.

Dividing by 10 – pages 144–145

If children struggle with division by 10, model it using counters. If necessary, point out that the digits move one place to the right, so that 20÷10 is 2. Use the strategy outlined above (*Dividing by 2*) of saying the 10s multiplication table, then the 10s division table: 10 divided by 10 is 1; 20 divided by 10 is 2…

Dividing by 3, 4 and 5 – pages 146–147

There are no visual clues to help with the division. If children find this difficult, they may like to use counters to share out. Alternatively, use a number line. For 12÷3, for example, count back in jumps of 3 from 12 to 0. Ask, 'How many jumps did we make? – so 12÷3 is 4.'

Finding remainders – pages 148–149

Children who need extra help with this activity could use counters to model the division and to find the remainder. Alternatively, use a number line and count back in equal jumps. For dividing 7 by 2, count back from 7 in 2s. The children will find that they will have a remainder of 1.

Halves and fourths – pages 150–151

This activity is designed to help children make the link between division and finding fractions of quantities. If they are unsure, suggest that they count out small even quantities of counters and to find half. When they are confident with this, count out quantities that can be divided by four, ask them to find half, then half again. Explain that this gives quarters.

Finding halves – pages 152–153

Where children know their 2 times table, they should be able to find halves quickly, deriving the half fact from a multiple of 2. Some of these numbers are multiples of 10. If children are unsure about finding their halves, use a number line to find 0 and the decade number. Suggest that they look for the mid-point. Talk about how, where the decade digit is odd, half will have a 5 in the units, and where it is even, it will have 0 in the units.

Fingers and thumbs – pages 154–155

This activity involves dividing by 10 to find the number of children. However, when including toes, the children will need to think about dividing by 10 and by 2. If they are unsure about this, model it with real fingers, thumbs and toes.

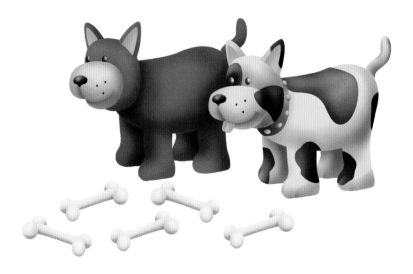

Suggestions for using this book

The illustrations are bright, cheerful, and colorful, and are designed to capture children's interest. Sit somewhere comfortable together as you look at the book. Children of this age will usually need to have the instructional words on the pages read to them.

Children are introduced to numbers up to 30, and then to numbers up to 100. They are encouraged to work both practically, by counting, and using counters or tokens, and by "counting in their heads."

Other activities include recall of addition and subtraction facts for all numbers up to 10, such as 3+6 and 9-1. Children can use what they know about addition to make totals of 100 using decade numbers, such as 60+40. They add and subtract tens and units using mental methods.

Early concepts associated with muliplication are also covered. Children identify odd and even numbers, count in 2s, 3s, 4s, 5s, and 10s and learn about arrays. Children will find it useful to use their knowledge about multiplication when dividing by sharing numbers into equal sets.

Encourage children to explain how they worked out the answers to the questions. Being able to explain their thinking, and to use the correct mathematical vocabulary, helps children to clarify in their minds what they have done. Also, when children are unsure of how to solve the problem, hearing what others did, and how they did it, helps them to use these methods more effectively.

At this stage, children will be beginning to write number sentences using +, −, x, ÷, and =. Encourage children to do this because it is a way of recording sums and can clarify the meanings of these abstract signs for the children.

Encourage children to make notes as they work at an activity. They can record numbers, writing them in order, or write simple sentences to explain. Encourage them to be systematic in the way that they work, so that they do not leave out a vital part of the evidence that they need to find a solution.

Some of the activities are games for two or more to play together. Play the game and make some "deliberate" mistakes. This will challenge children to spot the mistakes and to correct you. This will help you to assess how well they understand and can use the mathematical ideas that the pages are teaching.

Remember, learning about math should always be a positive experience. So enjoy together the mathematical games, activites, and challenges in this book.